PUPPY CARE & TRAINING

Teoti Anderson

Puppy Care & Training

Project Team
Editor: Stephanie Fornino
Copy Editor: Joann Woy
Design: Stephanie Krautheim

Series Design: Stephanie Krautheim and Mada Design
Series Originator: Dominique De Vito

T.F.H. Publications
President/CEO: Glen S. Axelrod
Executive Vice President: Mark E. Johnson
Publisher: Christopher T. Reggio
Production Manager: Kathy Bontz

T.F.H. Publications, Inc.
One TFH Plaza
Third and Union Avenues
Neptune City, NJ 0775

Printed and bound in China

ISBN 978-0-7938-3681-9

09 10 11 12 13   5 7 9 8 6

Library of Congress Cataloging-in-Publication Data
Anderson, Teoti.
  Puppy care & training / Teoti Anderson.
    p. cm.
  Includes index.
  ISBN 978-0-7938-3681-9 (alk. paper)
  1. Puppies. 2. Puppies--Training. I. Title. II. Title: Puppy care and training.
SF427.A673 2007
636.7'0887--dc22
                          2007000349

This book has been published with the intent to provide accurate and authoritative information in regard to the subject matter within. While every reasonable precaution has been taken in preparation of this book, the author and publisher expressly disclaim responsibility for any errors, omissions, or adverse effects arising from the use or application of the information contained herein. The techniques and suggestions are used at the reader's discretion and are not to be considered a substitute for veterinary care. If you suspect a medical problem consult your veterinarian.

The Leader In Responsible Animal Care For Over 50 Years!®
www.tfh.com

TABLE OF CONTENTS

PREPARING

for Your Puppy

Congratulations on your new family member! Add a puppy to your household, and your life will never be the same. Even if you've had other dogs before, each puppy is unique and brings her own personality and issues along in one furry package. She's going to charm you. She'll try your patience. She's going to challenge your ability to keep up with her. She's going to entertain you, aggravate you, and completely steal your heart.

When you're gazing into those soft, dark eyes, and hearing yourself coo baby talk that you didn't know you had in you, it's easy to forget that your new puppy is a different species. Some puppy owners want their puppies to be like little furry people, but don't sell your princess short! Dogs are very special creatures unto themselves. Understanding their special needs and motivations will go a long way toward helping you incorporate your puppy into your family for life.

Owning a puppy brings great responsibility. To do it right, it takes a lot of work. You'll want to keep her healthy and safe, housetrain her, teach her family manners, show her how to get along with all different types of people and other animals, and more. You may even have big plans for the future, like agility competition or therapy work or some other activity. Let's get your new family member on the right track right from the start.

PREPARING YOUR FAMILY

Preparing your family for the arrival of a new puppy is an important step. By making decisions in advance, assigning specific responsibilities, and prepping your children, your puppy will more easily adapt to the family routine.

Make Decisions in Advance

One of the best things that you can do for your puppy is to decide some things ahead of time with your family. Where is the puppy going to sleep? Will she be allowed on the furniture? Where is her potty area? Are there any areas of the house in which she won't be allowed? What will be her daily schedule?

Caring for a puppy is a lot of work, but it brings great rewards.

If you settle these questions ahead of time, your puppy's transition to her new home will be much smoother. For example, if you figured that she would sleep in your bedroom but your spouse thought that she would spend nights in the laundry room, you could have a problem. Also, you might have an issue if you don't want the puppy on the furniture, but your kids immediately let her up on the bed. Your dog will feel confused if everyone's not on the same page, and it will be harder to train her as a result. Settle these issues before bringing your puppy home so that everyone in your family has the same expectations.

Assign Responsibilities

Are different members of your family going to be responsible for different aspects of your new puppy's care? Be sure to lay out all responsibilities ahead of time so that everyone knows what to do. Be realistic. Some parents want their children to take primary responsibility for a puppy, but some kids just aren't old enough or ready for it yet. This is not the time to teach a child a lesson about not following through, because a living, breathing creature is part of the lesson. If a child is forgetful and dashes off to baseball practice without feeding the puppy, it's the puppy who will be hungry.

Instead, set your family up to succeed. Assign responsibilities that are truly realistic for each child. Show them what you expect, and make sure that they understand. To help to keep everyone on the same page, try creating a weekly chart for your family so that they can track their responsibilities. Post it in a place where everyone will see it often, like on the kitchen refrigerator.

Special Considerations for Children

If you have children, teach them ahead of time how to behave when the new puppy arrives. Puppies and children can be the best of friends, or they can terrify each other. It's natural for puppies to jump up, mouth everything with needle teeth, and bowl into little ones hard enough to knock them down. This can cause your children to be afraid of your new puppy. It's also natural for children to make loud noises, run, flail their hands, and not always understand how to be gentle. These kinds of behaviors can cause your puppy to be afraid of your children.

Here are some tips to help your kids and new puppy get along:

- Teach your children to walk, not run, when the puppy is present. Puppies will naturally chase a running child, especially if you have a herding breed.
- Teach your children to be quiet and still if the puppy jumps on them. Flailing hands and high-pitched wails are very exciting for a puppy and will probably rile her up more. Instead, teach your kids to stand still and wrap their arms around their bodies. Puppies will find this behavior less enticing, and they'll be less likely to jump up and nip.
- Teach your children to be kind and gentle with the puppy and never to tease her.

In return, you'll be teaching your puppy solid family manners so that she learns how to be gentle with your little ones, too.

PREPARING YOUR HOME

Puppies get into everything! This is why it's very important that you puppy-proof your home and eliminate any dangerous or tempting items that could cause your dog harm. You also should put away anything of value that you don't want her to chew.

You will eventually teach your puppy only to chew on appropriate items, but at first, she won't have a clue about what she's allowed to munch on or not. She's a baby, so she's exploring her world with her mouth. How big is your puppy? Get down on

Meeting the New Puppy

Everyone is bound to be excited about your puppy's arrival. Many new puppy owners want to invite everyone over to meet the new family addition right away. This could overwhelm your puppy; in fact, too many people crowding around her can cause her to be stressed or afraid. This will make a bad first impression and could cause her to be nervous around people. All that commotion also could get some puppies overexcited. Give your puppy a few days to settle into her new home and routine, then start inviting people over to meet her.

the floor at the same level your puppy will be—what do you see? Anything at puppy nose or eye level is fair game for chewing as far as your puppy is concerned. Also realize that this level will change as your puppy grows.

Common Puppy Temptations

Common puppy temptations include the following:

- **Items on the floor:** These include shoes, purses, umbrellas, remote controls, etc.
- **Toys:** If you have children who keep their toys all over the place, a puppy will find them irresistible. Teach your children to put their toys away before you bring a puppy home so that no one loses a precious teddy bear.

  Do you also have cats who have small toys? If you are bringing home a medium- or large-breed puppy, cat toys may be too small for her and could cause a stomach blockage should she swallow one. Pick up all small cat toys and keep them away from your puppy. Either keep them in a room that only your cats can access, or give your cats bigger toys to play with that also will be safe for your puppy.
- **Dangling items:** These include doilies on the coffee table, tassels on curtains, hand towels in the kitchen, leashes over the back of a chair, etc.

Common Household Dangers

Common household dangers include the following:

- **Electrical cords:** Be sure that they are tucked out of the way of your puppy's reach.
- **Some plants and flowers:** Azaleas, lilies, geraniums, philodendron, and other plants can be toxic. Check with your veterinarian if you have questions about any plants, flowers, or shrubs residing in your home and yard.
- **Human medicine:** Puppies will eat anything, and that includes any stray pills they may find. Many human medications are deadly to your puppy, so be sure to keep all drugs—prescription and over-the-counter—out of her reach.
- **Hosiery:** If your puppy swallows any kind of hosiery, it could become lodged in her digestive tract, with deadly results.
- **Dental floss, string, yarn, rubber bands, and holiday tinsel:** These also can cause intestinal blockage or strangulation.

Teach your child how to interact properly with a puppy.

- **Antifreeze:** If you have puddles of antifreeze in your driveway or garage, clean them thoroughly before your puppy arrives. Many antifreeze brands have an appealing smell and sweet taste to animals, but this substance is a deadly poison. Choose a brand for your vehicle that is marked safer for pets.
- **Cocoa mulch:** This can be toxic.

No matter how well you think that you've puppy-proofed your home, your puppy will find the one thing that you missed. It's hard to predict everything she'll get into, but do your best to minimize the damage. You'll also learn to keep a close eye on your puppy so that you can protect her and your belongings.

SUPPLIES

Have you ever picked up a catalog that sells dog products? You may have been amazed at the amount of stuff that's out there just calling to your credit card. From gourmet treats to shampoos to fancy dog beds, shopping for your puppy can be an adventure. You don't have to spend a fortune to make sure your puppy has a good start in life, though. In fact, there may be some items that you shouldn't splurge on until your puppy gets through the chewing stage. Your puppy will, however, need some basic supplies.

Baby Gate

Baby gates come in very handy with a puppy in the household. There will be times when you want to give your puppy more room than her crate allows, but she's not ready for the run of the house just yet. Baby gates allow you to conveniently close off part of your home. You also can use a baby gate to block the top or bottom of stairs or entrances to a deck or patio.

Baby gates are also a necessity if you have cats. It is normal for a young puppy to chase a cat. Until you teach her to leave your cat alone, you must manage the problem. Put a baby gate in the doorway to a "safe room" for your cat. Kitty will jump over the gate, but your puppy won't be able to follow. This will make your cat feel much safer. You also can use a baby gate to block off your cat's food and litter box. Puppies often love the taste of cat poop! Don't even give your puppy the chance to enjoy that icky delicacy; block off your cat's litter box so that your puppy can't get to it.

You'll find baby gates in children's areas of department stores and in pet supply stores. Some types bolt into the wall, while others are spring-loaded and don't require any installation hardware. They come in plastic, wood, and metal. You'll find extra-tall ones (in case you have a tall puppy) and some that even have cat doors. For convenience, you may want to look for a baby gate that features a swing door so that you don't have to step over it all the time.

A baby gate allows you to conveniently close off part of your home for your puppy's safety.

Bed

Beds come in all shapes, colors, sizes, and materials. Choose a size that will fit your puppy comfortably. Before you spend a lot of money on a quality bed, you may want to wait until your puppy is past her chewing stage, at around nine months. Otherwise, you may discover that she thinks the beautiful bed you bought her to nap on is much better for chewing! There are some chew-resistant beds on the market if you have a real power chewer. You also can spray the bed with chew deterrent spray. If your puppy insists on shredding her bed or crate pad, however, it's best to remove it altogether rather than risk her eating it and getting a stomach obstruction.

Choose a bed that will fit your puppy comfortably.

Chew Deterrent

You must watch your puppy closely to make sure that she doesn't chew on something inappropriate. You'll also teach her to leave certain items alone, and encourage her to chew on appropriate items. But your puppy is going to be tempted to chew on all sorts of things, so get some chew deterrent spray. Spray this bitter-tasting spray on items that you don't want your puppy to chew on, like plants and shoes. Most puppies do not like the taste, so they will avoid chewing on those items.

Some puppies don't seem to mind the taste of chew-deterrent

spray at all. If you have one of these, you'll have to get a bit creative. Try another brand of chew-deterrent spray or even some hot sauce (but make sure that it won't damage or stain the item first).

Cleaning Supplies

Puppies are messy. They are bound to have housetraining accidents in the house until you train them. Sometimes they vomit or have diarrhea, or they track in dirt and grass from outside. Be prepared for these messes by having a few cleaning supplies on hand when you bring your puppy home.

For housetraining accidents, choose a cleaner that has enzymes in it especially for pet messes. If you use a regular carpet or floor cleaner, vinegar, or other spot remover, your floor may look and smell clean to you, but it won't to your puppy. Her sense of smell is keener than yours, so she still may be able to smell where she has eliminated, which will encourage her to do it again on the same spot. Choose a pet enzymatic cleaner, and you'll avoid this problem.

Check your regular household cleaners to make sure that they are safe for use around puppies. For example, some aerosol disinfectant sprays can be harmful to your puppy. You may have been using it to clean your bathroom for years and might not be aware that it could pose a hazard to your new family member. Check with your veterinarian to find out if any of your regular household cleaners pose a problem.

Collar

A variety of collars are on the market that you can purchase for your puppy. A good collar to start with is a basic flat one with a buckle or a plastic quick-snap connector. The collar should fit snugly against your puppy's neck. When you slip your fingers in between the collar and her neck, you should only be able to get two flat fingers underneath the collar. You may worry that the collar is too tight, but having too loose a collar is dangerous. She could slip loose, or if her jaw becomes caught in the collar, she could panic and hurt herself.

Avoid choke chains, prong collars, or slip collars for your puppy. These can cause damage to your puppy's throat, and they are not necessary when you use modern, reward-based training methods.

To Have and To Hold

Everyone in your family should know how to properly pick up a puppy. Scoop one hand under your puppy's belly and lift, while quickly supporting her rear end with your other hand. Hold your puppy close to your chest, not out at arms' reach. This will make her feel safe, with less chance of a squirming puppy getting dropped.

Important: Remove your puppy's collar when she's in her crate. The collar or tags on the collar could get caught in the door or wire frame of the crate and cause her to choke.

Crate

A crate is a rectangular cage made of a variety of sturdy materials (such as plastic or wire) used to keep an animal confined. It's a very important tool for training your puppy. You can use a crate to:

- **Housetrain your puppy.** Most puppies will not soil their dens. By confining your puppy in a crate on a regular schedule (appropriate for her age and activity level), you'll be teaching her bladder and bowel control.
- **Keep your puppy safe.** Puppies will put just about anything in their mouths, including things that could hurt them. Confining your puppy in a crate when you can't supervise her closely will ensure that she isn't chewing or swallowing something dangerous.
- **Help your puppy heal should she become injured.** Hopefully, your puppy will grow up healthy and whole. But what if she injures a leg? Your veterinarian may tell you that you need to keep your puppy still for a certain period of time. This task is much easier to accomplish with a crate.
- **Travel with your puppy.** Puppies never should be loose in your car while you're traveling—there's too much risk that they could become injured if you have an accident. By putting your puppy in a crate and securing the crate to your vehicle's seat or floor, your puppy will be safely buckled up like the rest of your family.

How do you know what kind of crate to get? Some crates are better suited for certain purposes. For example, if you're trying to housetrain your puppy, it's best to get a crate that is just large enough for her to stand up, stretch out, and turn around in. Anything larger and she could urinate in a corner and stay dry all day, which will not help to teach her bladder control. As she grows older and you housetrain her, give her more room with a larger crate.

If you want a crate for traveling with your puppy, a wire crate that folds up suitcase style is a better choice than a canvas crate. The wire crate will be heavier than the canvas, but a young puppy

Tiny Dancers

Do you have a toy-breed puppy? It can be hard to find collars to fit the little ones. Try shopping online for stores that specialize in catering to small dogs. You can also try a cat collar—just make sure that it's not a breakaway collar, or your puppy could get loose.

A crate is an effective housetraining tool.

who is going through a chewing stage could chew right through the canvas.

Let's review the common types of crates, along with their advantages and disadvantages.

Plastic Crates

Plastic crates are very versatile. They're good for confinement and housetraining your puppy and convenient for travel. They come in a variety of colors and sizes and are usually less expensive than other types of crates. Many come in two parts—a top and bottom—that are connected by bolts and screws. This makes the crate easy to take apart for cleaning, although some plastic crates have raised sections in the bottom that can be awkward to clean. Be sure to tighten the screws regularly because they can become loose over time.

If you have a large-breed puppy, you may want to pass on a plastic crate unless you don't mind purchasing several to accommodate her change in size as she grows. If you get a large crate to start with, try to block a portion of it to make it smaller. Keep in mind, though, that your puppy may just chew on the item you use.

Plastic crates provide a limited view, which may be beneficial for some dogs. A shy puppy, for example, may feel safer in an enclosed den. A reactive puppy—one who barks at every little sight or sound—may be less likely to react to things that she can see from within the more limited view of a plastic crate.

If your puppy is a chewer, she may find the plastic irresistible. This can cause some rough edges. Try using some chew-deterrent spray to dissuade her from nibbling on her crate.

Wire Crates

Wire crates are also very versatile and are good for confinement, housetraining, and travel. They come in a variety of sizes and finishes—plain wire, epoxy-coated wire (which is more rust resistant), and more. These sturdy crates are usually appropriate for strong chewers. They feature a metal or plastic bedpan in the bottom that pulls out for easy cleaning. While this is convenient, if your puppy should become ill and have diarrhea or vomit, it could overspill the bedpan and go onto your carpet or floor.

Many wire crates come with dividers. This is very convenient if you have a large-breed puppy. You simply put the divider in to limit your puppy's space, then move it as she grows older.

Wire crates offer your puppy a better view than do most plastic ones. If she is shy, it may not feel as safe to her. If she is reactive, it also may make it too easy to see things that could trigger her barking. If you prefer a wire crate but find that the view is not working for your puppy, consider getting a crate cover. These fit over the tops and sides (but not the front) of a crate and come in a variety of fabrics to match your décor. Make sure that the cover does not get inside the crate or your puppy could chew on it.

The spacing between wires varies. Choose a crate that has holes small enough so that your puppy cannot catch her paws in them, or she could become tangled and injured.

Many wire crates fold up conveniently for storage or travel. If you get a "suitcase-style" wire crate it will have handles for carrying.

Canvas Crates

Canvas crates are great for confinement and travel, but they are not ideal for puppies who are not yet past the chewing stage. Puppies are teething at four to five months of age, and their back

Plastic crates are versatile and are appropriate for confinement, housetraining, and travel.

molars come in at around eight months. If you like the canvas crates, wait a while. Make sure that your puppy will not turn your investment into a chew toy!

Canvas crates can be harder to clean than other types of crates, because they're made of fabric. Some brands feature removable and replacement covers.

Soft-Sided Carriers

Soft-sided carriers are great for traveling. They're basically a small purse or piece of luggage with a shoulder strap for carrying. They are appropriate for toy or small-breed dogs. For short-term travel, a soft-sided carrier may be a convenient choice. Because they are not sturdy enough to resist chewing, however, they are not suitable for confinement or housetraining purposes.

Other Types of Crates

Because crate training has become so popular, a lot of other options are available to puppy owners. You'll see ads for wicker or rattan crates, and some that even double as beautiful solid wood furniture. If you want a crate that is fashionable as well as practical, be sure to pick a crate that's best for your puppy. For example, if your puppy is chewing, then a wicker or rattan crate will not hold up to puppy teeth. You may want to start with a more traditional type of crate and wait until your puppy is older or an adult before you splurge on a fashionable one.

Exercise Pen

An exercise pen is an enclosure made up of panels that fold up for travel or storage purposes. It is open at the top and bottom. Depending on the size and number of panels, exercise pens can be small or quite roomy.

If you travel with your puppy, an exercise pen is a real convenience. You can set it up and give your puppy a small, "fenced-in yard" to stretch her legs. It also can be a good transition from a crate—rather than giving your puppy the run of an entire room, you can see how she does with the greater freedom of an exercise pen first.

Food and Water Bowls

Walk down a pet supply store aisle of bowls and you'll find an array of dinnerware to rival any department store's china

All About Crates

Crate type:	Best uses:	Features:	Consider:
Plastic	• Puppy training • Adult dog training • Confinement • Housetraining • Travel	• Sturdy • Provides limited view • Can come apart for easy cleaning and transition to dog bed • Usually less expensive than others	• Nuts and screws may come loose • Some dogs will chew plastic • Some crates have raised sections on bottoms that can be awkward to clean • Some do not fold up for storage/travel (check brands) • May have to purchase larger crate as puppy grows
Wire	• Puppy training • Adult dog training • Confinement • Housetraining • Travel	• Sturdy • Durable, usually good for strong chewers • Provides good view • Many fold up for storage/travel • Bedpan pulls out for cleaning • Some feature dividers for growing puppies	• Some space between wires may be too big relative to puppy's size, which could catch paws and cause injury • If dog gets sick, could overspill bed pan • Usually more expensive than others
Canvas	• Adult dog training • Confinement • Travel	• Lightweight • Easy to set up/take down	• Not good for chewers • Surface not as easy to clean as others
Soft-sided carrier	• Travel	• Lightweight	• Best for small puppies only • Surface not as easy to clean as others

An exercise pen gives your puppy a safe place to play, especially while traveling.

department. Plastic bowls are lightweight and economical. They also harbor bacteria growth more than stainless steel bowls, and some puppies treat them like chew toys. Ceramic bowls come in a variety of patterns and are usually heavier, which can help to prevent a large puppy from pushing them across the floor as she eats. They also can easily chip or break. Stainless steel bowls are preferable because they do not promote the growth of bacteria as much as other types of bowls. They're also durable against puppy teeth, and some are even dishwasher safe, which is convenient.

In the past, many experts recommended that large-breed puppies be fed from a raised food bowl. The idea was that raised bowls aided digestion and prevented bloat, a deadly condition in which a dog's stomach fills with gas and twists, cutting off circulation. Immediate surgery to relieve the gas pressure is required or a dog could die. Recent research, however, does not support the use of raised food bowls. Purdue University School of Veterinary Medicine did a study that determined that raised bowls increased the incidence of bloat by 110%.

Do you have more than one dog? Each dog should have her own food bowl. This will help you to regulate how much food each dog receives. Teach your puppy to eat only from her own bowl and not to steal from anyone else's.

Grooming Supplies

The grooming supplies that you get for your puppy will depend a lot on what kind of puppy you have and what activities you plan for her. The requirements for grooming a Poodle, for example, are a lot more complicated than those for a Labrador Retriever. What you need to groom a puppy for the show ring may be very different from what you need for a puppy who's going camping with you.

For guidance on grooming supplies, consult your puppy's breeder and a professional groomer. They'll be able to give you tips specific to your particular puppy. In general, here are some basic tools you need. You'll find them at local and online pet retailers.

Brushes and Combs

The following are some brushes and combs that your puppy may need:

- **Slicker brush:** Slicker brushes remove dead fur and help with tangles. If you have a young puppy or a puppy with a very short coat, be sure to get a gentle slicker brush so that the bristles aren't painful.
- **Bristle brush:** Bristle brushes are good for puppies with all lengths of coats.
- **Pin brush:** Pin brushes are suitable for long-haired puppies; they have long, round-ended pins. You also may want to get a comb to help with potential tangles.
- **Stripping tool:** If you have a terrier or other harsh-coated puppy, you may want to get a stripping tool. This tool pulls out dead hair and keeps the coat wiry, which is the preferred look for a terrier. Clipping or trimming a terrier's coat makes it softer
- **Hound glove:** If you have a hound or other very short-coated puppy, consider getting a hound glove. This glove allows you to pet your puppy to comb through her coat.
- **Shedding blade:** If your puppy sheds, a shedding blade can be a tremendous help. This isn't a "blade" like a knife; rather, it is more like a comb. Most have short, serrated edges. You comb your dog with the shedding blade, and it strips out the dead fur.
- **Flea comb:** A flea comb is always handy. By using a flea comb and carefully going through your puppy's coat, you will help to ensure that you're trapping all the pesky parasites.

Coat Clippers and Scissors

Some puppies have coats that require clipping or cutting. Even if you choose to use the services of a professional groomer, you also may want to keep some clippers or scissors on hand for touch-ups between visits. A wide variety of clippers and attachments is available. If you're going to be clipping your puppy, check with your breeder or groomer for tips on what to purchase.

A pair of ear and nose hair scissors is invaluable. These have a small, blunt tip, just like safety scissors, so that you are less likely to painfully poke your puppy. If your puppy is fluffy and growing fur between her paw pads, use these scissors to keep that fur neatly trimmed. Small-sized electric clippers also do the trick.

Shampoos and Conditioners

Avoid shampoos formulated for humans because they may dry out your puppy's coat or skin. Instead, choose a shampoo that's especially formulated for your puppy. For example, does she have itchy, flaky skin? She may need a soothing oatmeal-based or medicated shampoo. Does she have a dry coat? She may do well with a conditioning shampoo or even a separate conditioner.

Some shampoos can enhance certain color coats. You'll find a variety of scented shampoos as well, some with organic ingredients. You'll also find some that kill fleas and ticks. If you're going to use a flea and tick shampoo, consult your veterinarian first if your dog is also using flea and tick prevention medication. You don't want to overload your puppy with chemicals, or she could get sick.

Bathing Extras

Your puppy may be small enough so that you can easily bathe her in a sink. If you have a larger puppy or a small puppy who's growing larger by the day, though, you may prefer to wash her in the bathtub. In this case, consider getting a faucet or shower extension attachment so that you can more easily rinse your puppy. Some are removable, while others attach permanently.

For extra drying power after the bath, try one of the special pet-drying towels. They absorb a lot more than regular bath towels and are machine washable.

Nail Care Items

There are different types of nail trimmers on the market. One type is the guillotine-style trimmer. You insert your puppy's nail into the opening, above the cutting blade. When you squeeze the handle, it pushes the blade, which cuts the nail. Some people prefer scissors-type nail trimmers. Other trimmers have safety mechanisms that limit the amount of nail you cut.

If you use a nail trimmer, your puppy's nails will be pretty sharp when you're done cutting them. Use a nail file to smooth the sharp edges. That way, her claws won't be so painful to you if she jumps on you or into your lap. You'll find files especially made for dog nails along with the rest of the grooming supplies at your local and online pet retailer.

If you want smooth nails from the start, try an electric nail grinder. This handheld tool has a rapidly revolving sandpaper head attachment that smoothes a nail down instead of cutting it.

Be sure to also stock some styptic powder or gel, which will help to stop bleeding just in case you nick the quick of your puppy's nail.

Dental Care Items

Dental care is an important part of keeping your puppy healthy. Use toothpaste specifically formulated for dogs. It comes in a variety of flavors, from mint to poultry.

Use a toothbrush or finger brush to apply the toothpaste; your choice depends on what type of puppy you have and your personal preference. With a very small puppy, the finger brush may be a tight squeeze in that little mouth. Some dog toothbrushes have two heads—one small and one large—which can be convenient for reaching all your puppy's teeth while her mouth is small, and also when she's larger. Or if you have two different-sized dogs in your home, one large and one small, each can use one head of the brush.

Your puppy's breeder and a professional groomer will be able to tell you what grooming supplies are appropriate for your particular puppy.

Halters and Harnesses

If your puppy really pulls hard on the leash, if she jumps on people a lot, or if she's a large, strong puppy and you're having difficulty walking her, you may find a head halter or harness helpful.

Head Halters

Canine head halters operate on the same principle as head halters for horses. A nose loop on the halter gives you greater control over your puppy's head. Control the head, control the puppy.

Head halters are not muzzles. Your puppy can still eat, give kisses, and drink while wearing a head halter.

Several different brands are available. Be sure that the person who sells you a head halter knows how to properly fit it. Your puppy may need some time to get used to having a loop over her nose. You can speed this along by offering her treats through the nose loop.

Harnesses

Harnesses are another popular option. If you have a flat-faced breed of dog such as a Pug or English Bulldog who has difficulty breathing in certain situations, a harness may be a better option than a regular collar because it doesn't go across your puppy's throat. A harness that has a hook in the back for a leash will not stop your dog from pulling. Think about what they hook Huskies up to sleds with—harnesses! Harnesses redistribute a dog's weight across the back and chest so that your puppy will actually pull more efficiently. If she has an issue with pulling on the leash, try one of the newer harnesses that feature a leash hook in front. These seem to teach puppies better "body sense" so that they don't pull as much as they do with regular harnesses.

Identification

All puppies need identification in case they are ever lost or stolen.

Tags

The most basic form of ID is a tag. A variety of styles and colors of tags are available from which to choose. You can get one that hangs from your puppy's collar. You also can get one that rivets to the collar itself, if you don't like the jangling noise a tag makes. (This is also a good choice for very small puppies who would be weighed down by a hanging tag.) The tag should have your puppy's name and your contact information. Be sure to include a phone number with voicemail that you check often, like for a cell phone. Also consider adding the word "reward!" It may offer an incentive should someone find your puppy.

Microchips

Ask your veterinarian about microchipping your puppy. A microchip is a small computer chip that is implanted under the skin between your puppy's shoulder blades. It's about the size of a grain of rice and has a unique code embedded in it. When scanned by a microchip reader, the code is displayed. You register the code with a company, providing them with your name and contact information. Several registration companies are available, with different prices and services; research them to find out which one best suits your preferences.

With the microchip, you will receive a special ID tag for your puppy's collar with a toll free phone number on it for your microchip registration service. When someone scans the chip, they can call the toll-free number and give the chip number. The registration service will then notify you that your puppy has been found.

A microchip is not painful for your puppy—once it's inserted, she won't even notice that it's there. Each year during your puppy's annual checkup, ask your veterinarian to scan the chip to make sure that it's still in place and working properly.

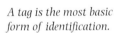

A tag is the most basic form of identification.

Tattoos

Tattoos provide another form of identification. Some people choose this option because they want a visible, permanent ID on their dogs. If your puppy is stolen, for example, it will be easier to prove she is yours if there's a mark on her that connects her to you. The tattoo is usually on a dog's inside haunch, although some puppies, like those raised for service work, get tattoos in their ears. Choose a number that is unique to you, and a professional will tattoo it onto your puppy. Some registration companies that track microchips also will allow you to register a tattoo number in your puppy's profile.

The ideal time to have this done is when your dog is under anesthesia. For example, when you neuter your puppy, ask your veterinarian to tattoo her at the same time. Anesthesia is not necessary for tattooing, but keep in mind that it can be a scary experience for your puppy to be tattooed while she's awake. If several people have to hold her still, and someone comes at her with a loud machine that pokes her with a needle, she could be badly frightened. The procedure may even cause her to be afraid of people. So, if you're interested in tattooing your puppy, talk to your vet to determine the best way to go about it.

If you choose to get your puppy tattooed without anesthesia, choose the person performing the procedure carefully. He should have experience performing the procedure, especially with impressionable puppies. Look for someone who is professional, friendly, and patient with your dog. Give your puppy plenty of treats throughout the procedure. Don't fuss over her—this could make her even more afraid. Instead, calmly reassure her and act upbeat. The tattooing shouldn't take long. Your goal is just to make the procedure as pleasant as possible.

Leash

Get your puppy a 4- to 6-foot (1.2- to 1.8-m) cotton, nylon, or leather leash. Don't allow her to chew on her leash. If she's persistent, spray it with a chew deterrent.

Don't use a retractable leash to train your puppy. They're bulky to hold when training, and they always keep tension on your puppy's collar. If your puppy gets used to this sensation, she may learn to pull when she's on a regular leash to keep that same tension. After your puppy has learned not to pull on leash, a retractable leash may not be so confusing. They are good for exercising your puppy, especially if you don't have a fenced yard.

Toys

Puppies have an instinctive need to chew. They also explore their environments mouth first. Toys can help to prevent destructive behavior. If your puppy is happily chewing on a toy, she's not tearing up your couch. Just because a toy is made specifically for dogs, however, doesn't mean that your puppy knows that. To her, your couch looks pretty tempting! It's up to you to teach her to chew on the right things.

The types of toys that you purchase for your puppy will depend on what kind of chewer she is. Some puppies will treasure a toy for years, while others will rip through them in seconds. Always choose a toy that is the proper size for your puppy. She should never be able to get the entire toy in her mouth. For example, a Golden Retriever puppy should not be allowed to play with golf balls. She could easily swallow them, which could require emergency surgery. Tennis balls are a much safer option for this puppy. Sometimes, chew toys start out the right size but don't last that way. If your puppy is wearing down a chewbone, always throw it away before she gets it down to a nub.

Some toys may be strong enough to leave your puppy with unattended. Other toys are not as tough and should never be allowed with your puppy unless you're keeping close watch. It depends on how tough your chewer is. Always err on the side of caution. If you're not sure that she should be left alone with a toy, don't take a chance.

When you choose a toy for your puppy, always keep in mind what you are teaching her. If you tie a knot in an old sock and give it to your puppy, it will be really cute until she starts chewing the socks on your feet! You won't be able to get angry with her, because you taught her it was okay to chew socks. If you give her an old shoe you were about to throw away, you're teaching her to chew shoes. Your puppy will not know the difference between the old shoe you were going to discard and the brand-new pair in your closet. Also, beware of toys that look like common household items. Some toys on the market look just like shoes, for example. If you give your puppy these fake shoes, she probably will not be able to distinguish them from the real ones.

This also goes for stuffed animals. Many pet retailers sell stuffed animals created especially for dogs, such as those made by Nylabone. If you choose to get these for your puppy, keep in mind that you are teaching her that it's okay to chew on stuffed animals. So, if you have children in your life—or plan to have kids—then be aware that your puppy will likely chew on their stuffed toys, too. It won't be her fault if she shreds your daughter's teddy bear, because you'll have taught her the behavior. If you don't have any other stuffed animals in your home, or if your kids will always put their toys up and away from puppy's reach, then choosing stuffed animals as a toy is not an issue.

Here are some common types of toys that most puppies enjoy:

Balls

Some puppies become obsessed with balls, while other puppies

Troubleshooting

If your puppy growls over a food-stuffed toy, or if you have more than one dog at home and they growl, snap, or fight over the toy, call a professional trainer or applied animal behaviorist for help. You should not let the dogs "work it out" among themselves, or one could get seriously hurt. In the meantime, avoid using a food-stuffed toy until a professional can assess the situation.

Choose a ball that is durable enough for your puppy's chewing habits.

couldn't care less. Balls come in all shapes and sizes, so choose one that is durable enough for your puppy's chewing habits. Be careful of balls designed for people, like ping pong balls or golf balls. These are too small for many puppies and could become lodged in your puppy's throat or cause a stomach obstruction if swallowed. Tennis balls are usually fine because they are larger. Some manufacturers make tennis-type balls just for dogs. If you have a giant-breed puppy, however, even a tennis ball may be too small. Just be sure that the ball is not so small that it fits entirely in your puppy's mouth.

Bones

Always choose a bone that your puppy cannot fit entirely in her mouth. If she wears it down, throw it away.

Quite a buffet of bones is available for your puppy to sink her teeth into, including:

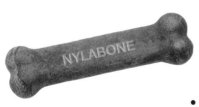

- **Real bones.** Don't give your puppy bones from your leftover dinner. Instead, purchase bones made specifically for dogs. For example, hollow beef marrow bones can be fun for your puppy to chew, plus you can stuff them with peanut butter, cheese, and other treats. Make sure that they are durable and that your puppy can't splinter off large pieces. Get the proper size for your puppy.
- **Rawhide bones.** As your puppy chews on rawhide, she will break off pieces and swallow them. Rawhide can be very difficult for your puppy to digest. Some puppies do fine with rawhide chews, while others experience digestive upsets. Some puppies also tear through rawhides very quickly. If the bone is too small, it could choke her.
- **Edible bones.** Some chew bones are made up of edible materials and are designed for your puppy to chew and consume. They are safe for your puppy to eat completely, and they come in a

variety of flavors. Look for edible bones without any plastics in them.

- **Nylon/plastic/rubber bones.** These are more durable alternatives to rawhide bones. Some come in softer textures for young or small-breed puppies, while others are really tough for power chewers. Choose one that matches your puppy's chewing habits. Some are plain, and some have flavorings added for greater appeal. Nylabone makes a variety of these types of toys that are suitable for a puppy's size and chewing power.
- **Rope bones.** Some puppies love to chew and toss rope bones. Some puppies will undo the knots, so you'll need to keep close watch. If your puppy undoes a knot, throw the rope bone away. Some puppies also like to pull the shredded ends of rope bones, and if they swallow the strings, it could be dangerous. If your puppy likes to do this, try trimming the ends very close to the knot so there will be less to pull. If this doesn't seem to work, choose another toy.

Toys for Stuffing

Some toys are made for stuffing with peanut butter, treats, and other food items. These are wonderful toys to occupy your puppy, and they also can be great rewards. When you leave your puppy in her crate, give her a food-stuffed toy to amuse her while she's confined. If you have company over, give your puppy a food-stuffed toy to keep her occupied while you greet your guests.

A food ball is one type of stuffing toy. As your puppy rolls the ball around, the food falls out. The more the food falls out, the more she will roll it around. If your puppy is chasing a food ball around the living room, she won't be chewing on your furniture!

Some toys for stuffing are made of hollow, durable rubber. These are excellent pacifiers for your chewing puppy. Put in a layer of peanut butter, then some of her kibble. You also can put in baby carrots or another healthy treat. Top it off with more peanut butter, then wedge a larger treat in the opening. If she becomes an expert at unstuffing her toy, try stuffing it and then freezing it before giving it to her.

Tug Toys

Choose a durable tug toy that will only be used for this purpose. Tug-of-war is not the evil game that some people have come to

Toy Rotation

Some puppy owners are surprised when their puppy still manages to chew on something inappropriate, despite the number of toys readily available. Remember, puppies are easily distracted and easily tempted. If your puppy sees a multitude of toys every day, sooner or later they'll begin to bore her. To keep her interested, rotate the toys so that she won't get so used to them. Put half the toys away. In a couple weeks, bring those toys out for your puppy while you put the current ones away. If you keep the toys rotated, they'll stay fresher to her longer.

believe. It actually can be a healthy outlet for your dog's instinctive predatory nature. Rather than chasing your cat, for example, you can teach her to play a safe game of tug with you. It's also a good energy and calorie burner. Puppies, especially sporting, terrier, herding, and other breeds, need a great deal of exercise. If you don't exercise your puppy enough, she may bounce off the walls, chewing everything in sight and generally acting like a child who's been cooped up all summer.

Tug-of-war goes wrong only when you don't set clear, consistent rules for playing the game. You don't want to teach your puppy to tug on everything she gets her jaws on or that it's okay to accidentally grab *you* instead of the toy. You must set up safe parameters for the game so that it remains a fun, healthy outlet. It's also not a good idea to play tug-of-war if your puppy shows signs of aggression. If she growls or snaps at you for any reason (for example, over her food bowl or a prized toy, when you try to pick her up, or if you try to brush her), don't play this game without supervision from a professional dog trainer or applied animal behaviorist. Please call for professional help before this problem gets worse.

Tug toys can help your puppy expend excess energy and burn calories.

Noisy Toys

Some dog toys have squeakers, some make animal noises, and some even let you record your own voice. Some puppies get wildly excited over squeaky toys. They can be a good way to redirect your puppy's attention. For example, if she's about to chew on something inappropriate, squeak a toy and call her to you.

Some shy puppies may be frightened of noisy toys; if that's the case with your dog, choose a different toy. You want her toys to be fun, not frightening! Also, keep close watch on the sound mechanism—some puppies become experts at "de-squeaking" a toy. If they swallow a squeaker, they may require emergency surgery.

Puzzle Toys

Puzzle toys have different parts that your puppy can pull apart. Some are larger toys with smaller toys inside it for her to pull out.

Preparing for your new puppy can be exciting, but it can put a dent in your checking account. Once you see all the equipment, toys, and *stuff* that's available, you tend to want more! Start with the basics described in this chapter for now. You and your puppy will both develop preferences as she grows, so you can tailor her supplies to what works best for both of you.

Chapter

2

BRINGING HOME
Your New Puppy

The big day has arrived! You are about to bring home your new family member. Are you ready?

THE RIDE HOME

Bring some treats and a toy. Also, bring a spare towel and some cleaning supplies in case your puppy gets carsick or has an accident on the way home.

You may be tempted to cuddle your new puppy on the ride home, but please resist the urge. Just as all your family members should wear their seatbelts in a moving car, your puppy also should be safely restrained—and your arms are no safety guarantee. Would you carry a baby home from the hospital in your lap? Of course not. To transport your puppy safely, use her crate for her first ride home. Surely, your need to cuddle that cute little fluffball is not as important as keeping her safe and secure. Getting her used to riding in the car properly will also be one of your first training opportunities.

If possible, have an adult friend or family member go with you so that you can keep your puppy company while the other person drives. Secure her crate in the backseat of your car. Put her in her crate, and give her a treat and the toy. Sit next to her so that you can talk to her while the other person drives. If she's being good, occasionally give her a treat. Don't overdo the treats at this time because she could become carsick. You can slip your fingers through the crate door to scratch her instead.

If your puppy is not used to being in a crate, she may whine or cry. Do not reassure her, because this will inadvertently reward the behavior and could make her more anxious. Just talk to her calmly. Try to redirect her attention to the toy. Be strong! Do not let her out of the crate, or you will be teaching her that crying works. Just as you wouldn't let a small child get out of a car seat because she complained, you shouldn't let your puppy out of her crate, either. Remember, her safety is a priority. Should you have an accident, you never would forgive yourself if she were thrown around inside the car or through a windshield.

If your ride home will take a couple hours or longer, you may need to stop to give your puppy a potty break. Avoid areas where other dogs have been because your puppy is very

Your puppy should be safely restrained in a crate on the ride home from the breeder's.

susceptible to diseases until she has had all her vaccinations. Instead of rest stops with designated pet areas, it's safer to stop at a fast-food place or other store and use a grassy area there. Always pick up after your puppy.

Carry her to the potty area rather than letting her walk. Bring pet or baby wipes with you to thoroughly wipe her paws after she's been on public grounds. Also, always make her wear a collar with identification, and take it off before putting her back in her crate. If you have an exercise pen, set that up for her as a potty area. If not, always make her wear a leash.

If she's not used to her collar and leash, she may stop to scratch her neck or react to them. Distract her, and don't be tempted to take them off if she complains. Safety first!

THE ARRIVAL

When you get home, immediately take your puppy to her potty area because she may have to relieve herself. Go ahead and start your housetraining right from the start.

If you have a fenced-in area, carry her there. If you do not have a secure yard, put on her collar and leash. Don't risk her dashing off—puppies are fast! Plus, you don't want her to learn her very first day that she can run away from you. Because she doesn't know you very well, you might have trouble catching her.

Don't be surprised if your puppy doesn't eliminate. She may be too excited, and this is normal. Give her about five minutes, then take her inside to her new home.

THE FIRST FEW DAYS

The first few days are the honeymoon period. You and your family will be completely entranced at your new family addition, and your puppy will provide you with hours of entertainment. You'll take pictures and e-mail your friends, you'll laugh at her cute antics…and you'll also start to realize just how much work raising a puppy can be.

Puppies need constant supervision. You may find that your

puppy has lots of energy but you're beginning to get very tired. Here are some tips for making the first few days easier:

- **Take your puppy to the vet right away.** Bring your puppy to the veterinarian within 48 hours to make sure that she is healthy and so that you can start her health care program.
- **Set rules now, and stick to them.** If you let your puppy get up on the couch with you now because she's small and cute but don't want her to get up there later when she's bigger, that will confuse her. Give her consistent structure.
- **Begin your training now.** Start teaching your puppy manners today, such as sitting for her food or at the door. If you train her now, she will keep those manners as she gets older. Puppies are like sponges—they soak up information. They have very short attention spans, though, so shorter training sessions are best.
- **Stick to a schedule.** Puppies do best with consistent routines. Even if you are home for a few days, you should keep your dog's feeding and potty schedules consistent, just as you would during the days you work.
- **Get your puppy used to being alone.** If you picked up your puppy on a weekend or decided to take a few days off to bond with her, she might be confused and upset the day you head back to work. To prevent this reaction, train her to being confined in her crate now. Leave her crated while you run short errands so that she won't experience such a dramatic transition when you return to your regular schedule.

Some puppies will waltz into your home and act like they've lived there all their lives. Some puppies may be hesitant or confused. Some puppies will be fine during the day, but whine or cry at night. Keep in mind that your puppy has left the only home she's known, and this could be a confusing transition for her. It may take her a couple weeks to feel comfortable and fit in with her new routine; this is normal.

If your puppy is very shy, if she hides from you, if she growls at you when you try to touch her or pick her up, or if she growls over her food bowl, call a professional, reward-based dog trainer. Your puppy may need special help.

MULTIPLE-PET HOUSEHOLDS

If you have other pets, you may be worried about how they will accept the new puppy. How do you let them know that you still

Make Sure You're Attached

Many puppy owners make the mistake of letting their puppies off leash outside during their first weeks together. Very young puppies are like little ducklings and will follow you around loyally. They're still kind of clumsy and can't move very fast. But this stage will disappear overnight. One day, the puppy who was sticking to you like glue will suddenly dash across the street, and no amount of calling will get her to come to you. This is not what you want to teach her. Don't give her the opportunity to run away from you, and you won't have to worry about chasing her. Set her up for success right from the start by putting her on a leash.

love them, even when there's a new addition to the household? In general, most animals can get along fine if introduced and managed properly.

Other Dogs

If your existing dog has a history of any kind of aggression with other dogs, call a professional dog trainer. Some people think that the perfect puppy makes an aggressive dog less aggressive, but this is rarely the case. Your new puppy could be seriously injured if your existing dog has problems with other dogs. A professional dog trainer can help you evaluate the situation and assist you in determining what's best for your family.

If your existing dog is fine with other dogs, then proceed with the introductions. If you have more than one dog, do introductions separately. When you first bring your puppy home, put your existing dog in a separate room. When you're ready to introduce them, have them meet in a neutral area, such as a neighbor's yard. (Make sure that the yard is safe for your puppy.) Both dogs should be on leash, with a different person managing each dog.

Bring your puppy to the vet within 48 hours of acquiring her to make sure that she is healthy.

Let them sniff each other. Try to hold the leashes loosely so that they don't sense any tension from you. If either dog becomes too excited, call them apart. Praise both dogs for good behavior. If things go well, bring them home.

Do not leave the dogs alone together unsupervised. Puppies can be relentless with older dogs. Some older dogs will discipline puppies. They may growl or snap at them, which is their way of teaching them canine manners. This is fine, as long as it doesn't escalate into injury. Other older dogs won't discipline a puppy at all. The bottom line is that you always should be in control of the situation. If you see your new puppy pestering your older dog, redirect the puppy's behavior. Don't let your older dog get nagged so much that she becomes stressed or unhappy.

Don't allow your puppy to steal your other dog's toys from him or eat from his food bowl. Don't let your older dog take all the puppy's things, either. You are the leader in your household, so it's up to you to maintain manners for all parties. Give each dog individual attention so that everyone feels loved.

If you see your new puppy pestering your older dog, redirect the puppy's behavior.

Cats

If your cat has had positive experiences with other dogs, introductions will go more easily. In any case, the key to success with cat–dog introductions is to go slowly. It's best to keep them apart for several weeks and gradually get them used to each other.

Manage the situation so that your cat is kept elsewhere when your puppy is loose, and so that the cat can be loose when your puppy is in her crate. Rub a towel over your puppy, especially on her paws, and leave it with your cat so that she becomes accustomed to your puppy's scent. Rub a towel on your cat, especially on her cheeks, and leave it with your puppy so that she gets used to kitty's scent as well.

After a week or two, introduce the pets in person. Always keep your puppy on leash. Keep your cat's nails trimmed short—cats have been known to swat at puppies and can cause injury, especially to the eyes. Praise both pets for good behavior. Don't force your cat to approach your puppy or hold her up next to your puppy. Let her approach at her own pace. If she chooses not to, keep up the management routine and try again later.

As they gradually become accustomed to one another without incident, make sure that things continue to go smoothly. Set up

Big and Little

Big and small dogs can be great friends, but you must be extra careful. A big dog could accidentally hurt a tiny puppy. A big puppy could easily injure an older small dog.

If you are introducing very different-sized dogs, hold the smaller dog at first. Praise the larger dog for being gentle. If the larger dog is a puppy or an adult dog who hasn't been trained, she will not automatically know how to be gentle with her new small friend. You will have to train her.

Never leave large and small dogs together unsupervised. A cry from a small dog could trigger the large dog to instinctually attack, even if they've been living together for a long time. If there are ever any signs of growling over toys or food, call a professional dog trainer.

baby gates so that your cat can have a safe escape route if necessary. Don't let your puppy chase your cat or play with her roughly. If necessary, tether her to you until you can teach her the *leave it* cue. (To learn how to train this cue, see Chapter 5.) Don't let your cat terrorize your puppy, either. Stay in control, manage their interactions, and you'll have a happy multi-species household.

Other Pets

If you have other pets, such as guinea pigs, rabbits, or horses, take your time in introducing your puppy. Set realistic expectations. For example, if you have a terrier puppy, it may be difficult to stop her from chasing a pocket pet, and she could injure or kill it. Always manage interactions to keep everyone safe.

CHOOSING A BOARDING KENNEL OR PET SITTER

Now that your puppy is settling into her new home, what if you have to leave her for an extended time? Maybe you planned a vacation before realizing you'd have a puppy in the household. Or maybe you have holiday plans to visit the family out of town, and a puppy wouldn't be welcome at the festivities. Or sometimes, traveling with a puppy just isn't in her best interests; long car rides, trying to find a hotel that allows dogs, a vacation where she won't get much attention— sometimes it's best to just leave your puppy at home.

Many new puppy owners overlook the need to find a quality pet sitter or boarding kennel well in advance of any travel plans. If you ever have to go out of town and leave your puppy behind, you cannot wait until the last minute to choose the right people to care for her. It's important to do your research ahead of time and always make reservations early. Good pet sitters are in hot demand, and quality boarding kennels fill up quickly! During holidays, especially, you may have to reserve a pet sitter or boarding kennel months ahead of time.

Introduce your puppy to your resident dog gradually to help them become accustomed to one another.

Why should you use a professional? While it's great if you can get a neighbor or friend to check in on your puppy during the day for a potty break, for example, that's usually just a half-hour visit. If you are gone for a weekend or a week, that's a longer commitment to ask of them. You also want someone who is prepared and qualified to handle medical emergencies or other issues that may arise.

Boarding Kennels

Kennels are a good choice for keeping dogs in a safe, confined area while you are traveling. However, they can be stressful places for puppies because they are unfamiliar and often quite loud. This is why it's important to find the right one to take care of your puppy.

Before considering leaving your puppy at a boarding kennel, she should have completed her immunizations, including the kennel cough vaccine. This will help to protect her against catching deadly diseases.

Here's how to narrow your search:

- Ask for recommendations from your veterinarian, dog trainer, and friends.
- Learn if your state requires boarding kennel inspections. If it does, make sure that the kennel you are researching displays the proper licenses or certificates.
- Check with your Better Business Bureau to see if any complaints have been registered about the kennel.
- Ask if the kennel belongs to the American Boarding Kennel Association (ABKA), a trade association that promotes professional standards of pet care.
- Ask if the kennel offers references from other clients.

Once you've narrowed down your list, it's time to schedule a visit. If the kennel doesn't allow tours, remove it from your list. How can you leave your puppy at a place you haven't seen? When you take your tour, here are some questions to keep in mind:

- Does the kennel require vaccinations? Even if your puppy has all her shots, you don't want to expose her to a kennel that doesn't have strict standards about health practices.
- Is the staff friendly to both you and your puppy? Is it knowledgeable?
- Is the kennel clean?
- Is it a comfortable temperature? If you live in an area with extreme temperatures, is there a contingency plan in case the power goes out?
- Will your puppy's kennel be roomy enough for her size? If you want her to share a kennel with another one of your dogs, is that allowed? (You should make sure that the dogs are safe to remain together well before kenneling.)
- Is it an indoor kennel or indoor/outdoor? If outdoor, is the area protected from the elements?
- Is there a schedule for exercise? Are puppies exercised individually or allowed to play with other boarders? Beware of kennels that will turn your puppy loose with dogs you don't know. Is there an expert on canine behavior on staff to determine if dogs are safe playmates and who supervises the play at all times? Puppy playtime may sound like a good exercise option, but it's also a good way for your puppy to get injured, have unpleasant dog socialization experiences, and develop behavior problems.

- Is bedding provided, or do you have to bring your own? Is bedding cleaned if it becomes soiled?
- How often will your puppy be fed? Can you bring her own food? This is important if she has food allergies.
- What veterinary services are available, including those outside regular veterinary office hours? If a problem occurs, will the kennel consult your puppy's veterinarian, or does it use another veterinarian?
- What other services are available, such as grooming or bathing? You may want your puppy bathed right before you pick her up.
- If training services are available, are they reward-based? How does the kennel deal with problem puppy behavior? For example, if your puppy jumps on a staff member, you don't want him kneeing your puppy in the chest to get her off or spanking her. Do all staff members follow reward-based methods of training?
- How much do they charge? Be sure to ask for ancillary service charges, because you may be surprised to learn that there may be extra charges for dispensing medication, taking your puppy out for a walk, feeding special food, and other services. Some kennels offer special perks, like televisions for the dogs or webcams for owners to see how their puppy is faring.
- How can you check on your puppy? Are there specific times

Kennels are a good choice for keeping dogs in a safe, confined area while you are traveling.

you need to call? Can you e-mail?

If possible, before taking a long vacation, try to leave your puppy at the kennel for a shorter period, such as a weekend. This will help to get her used to the experience, and you can troubleshoot any problems before taking your long trip.

Pet Sitters

If your puppy hasn't had all her shots yet, she shouldn't stay in a boarding kennel. Plus, she may feel more comfortable in her own environment.

A professional pet sitter will come to your home and feed, care for, and exercise your puppy. A pet sitter also usually provides additional services, such as bringing in your mail, watering plants, turning lights on and off, and generally checking on your home. Travel aside, you may want to consider hiring a pet sitter who offers a midday potty break service for young puppies. It could be well worth the money you'd save in gas and time away from work.

Some pet sitters come to your home for specific visits. Ideally, you should arrange to have the sitter come three times a day for your puppy. Some pet sitters also offer live-in services, meaning that they move into your home while you're away.

Here's how to narrow your search for a quality pet sitter:

- Ask for recommendations from your veterinarian, dog trainer, and friends.
- Check with your Better Business Bureau to see if any complaints have been registered about the pet sitter.
- Ask if the pet sitter belongs to any professional organizations, such as the National Association of Professional Pet Sitters (NAPPS) or Pet Sitters International (PSI).
- Ask if the pet sitter offers references from other clients.

Once you have your list, it's time to meet the pet sitters and find a good match for your puppy. Here are some questions to ask:

- Is she bonded and insured?
- Does she offer a written contract that explains services and fees?
- What kind of training has she had? What continuing education has she pursued? You want a pet sitter who is knowledgeable about canine behavior, basic medical care, and first aid.

Kennels and the Shy Puppy

Kennels are not an ideal choice for shy or fearful puppies because the environment may be too stressful for them.

- Can she handle special needs, such as giving medication?
- What are her procedures for a medical emergency? Will she contact your veterinarian, or does she use a specific veterinarian? What if an incident happens after regular veterinary office hours?
- What is the pet sitter's backup plan should she become ill or have an emergency and be unable to care for your puppy?
- How does she deal with problem puppy behavior? You don't want a pet sitter who will use harsh methods with your puppy. Do all staff members follow reward-based methods of training?
- What documentation will she provide detailing her visits?
- If you should be delayed arriving home, what would be the contingency plan? Could she continue taking care of your puppy until you returned?
- What are the charges? Are there additional charges for other services, such as watering plants or walking your puppy? If you have other pets, are there additional charges for caring for them?

Always arrange for a potential pet sitter to come to your home ahead of time so that you can meet her in person. Is she friendly, professional, and knowledgeable? How does she interact with your puppy? If everyone gets along and you are pleased with the interview, consider using her services for a short trip, such as over a weekend, before taking a longer vacation.

This is just the beginning. Now that your puppy is safe and sound in her new home, it's time to set up feeding and potty schedules and begin her family manners training.

Ask a potential pet sitter to come to your home so that you can see how she interacts with your puppy.

C h a p t e r

3

FEEDING

Your Puppy

I f you ate nothing but junk food, what would you be like? Probably cranky, with health problems ranging from high cholesterol to obesity to heart disease. Feed your puppy the equivalent of canine junk food and that will describe her, too. What your puppy eats will affect her health and behavior.

In general, you will pay more for higher-quality food. Is it worth it? Yes. If you pay more for what goes into your puppy, you'll likely pay less in veterinary and medication bills because your puppy will be healthier. She will have a better coat and skin, and be less likely to be irritable or hyperactive.

At first, it's best to feed your puppy whatever she was eating before you brought her home, at least for a few days. Do your research on food, and should you decide to switch, do so gradually, over the course of a week or so. If you switch foods on her suddenly, you could upset her stomach.

READING THE LABEL

Dog food can be a controversial subject. Those who favor certain diets or brands are sometimes critical of those who choose another. With so many types of foods and diets, so many brands, and so many competing sales pitches, how do you know what's best for your puppy? Learn how to read food labels so that you can understand exactly what you're feeding her.

Start with the list of ingredients. The law requires pet food manufacturers to list ingredients by weight. So if an item is listed first, that means there is more of that item in the food than the other items listed farther down the list. You want high-quality, easily digestible foods listed at the top. Be careful of manufacturers who split up an ingredient into several different smaller ingredients. For example, let's say at the top of the list you see "chicken, ground corn, corn gluten, corn bran." Three of those ingredients are corn. Put together, they may outweigh the top ingredient—chicken. There is also a difference if the manufacturer uses human-grade ingredients. A cheaper brand of dog food may have a deceptively good ingredient list, but if the food is not human grade, then there is less quality going into your puppy.

Puppies who eat a high-quality food absorb more of the nutrients, so there is less stool. (That's less for you to pick up!)

BASIC NUTRIENTS

There can be a lot of things listed on a dog food label. Are all of them really necessary for your puppy's health? Start by understanding the basic nutrients that your puppy needs for good health.

Proteins

Protein is one of the most important nutrients in your puppy's diet. Identifying good proteins is a way to differentiate between quality dog foods and poor ones. The building blocks that make up protein, called *amino acids*, are necessary for your puppy's growth and development and play an important role in her immune system.

Meat is a desirable protein. Look for meat as the first ingredient on your food label's list, but realize that there are different levels of meat quality. The highest quality is plain meat, such as chicken or lamb. The next level of meat is meal, such as chicken meal or lamb meal. The next level of meat is by-products, such as turkey by-products, chicken by-products, or lamb by-products.

In general, puppies need higher amounts of protein than do adult dogs. Some debate exists about how much is necessary, though. Some researchers believe that high-protein diets can interfere with a dog's ability to absorb tryptophan, an amino acid that helps the body produce serotonin. Serotonin is a chemical that acts as a calming agent in the brain. If you have a fearful or aggressive puppy, or if you find that she is very hyper, you may want to consider feeding her a lower amount of protein. In general, puppies do well with 21 percent to 28 percent protein. Very high-protein diets (35 percent to 40 percent) are for working dogs and are not necessary for the average household puppy.

Carbohydrates

Carbohydrates give your puppy energy. Common carbohydrates

A balanced diet contributes to your puppy's overall health.

in puppy food are rice, millet, barley, corn, and oats. Be wary of dog foods that list carbohydrates first in their lists of ingredients or that use them as fillers. Dog foods with a lot of carbohydrates also can lead to obesity because your puppy will store the excess as fat in her body.

Fats

Your puppy needs fats to be healthy. If she doesn't get enough fat, she could get dandruff and a dry coat. There is such a thing as too much, however. Too much fat in her diet could lead to pancreatitis, a severe and sometimes life-threatening disease.

Look for ingredients that list specific fats, such as flaxseed oil, rather than just "animal fat."

Vitamins and Minerals

Vitamins and minerals help with digestion, muscle and bone growth and function, healthy skin and fur, the metabolism of fats, proteins, and carbohydrates by the body, and more.

Water

Water is necessary for life. Always make sure that your puppy has access to fresh, clean water. Wash her water bowl daily with warm, soapy water.

TYPES OF FOOD

Your puppy can get her daily nutrients in a variety of ways. If you head down a pet supply store's dog food aisle, you'll soon discover a dizzying selection of bags, cans, packets, and other containers, all vying for your attention. Some people choose to bypass the store altogether and make their puppy's food at home. Which is best for your puppy? Learn about the different types of food, along with their advantages and disadvantages.

Commercial Diets

Commercial dog food diets come in three main types: dry, canned, and semi-moist.

Dry Food

Advantages: Dry food or kibble is very common and easily available. It may assist in good dental hygiene, scraping plaque and tartar off the teeth if the puppy has to chew it significantly. Dry food is usually less expensive per pound (kg) than canned food. It has greater caloric density than does canned food, so puppies need to eat less to get the nutrition they need.

Disadvantages: Some finicky puppies turn their nose up at dry food, but this is more common if you've fed your puppy table scraps or started out with canned food.

Canned Food

Advantages: Canned foods are very tasty to puppies. Depending on ingredients, higher amounts of fat could improve skin and coat. Canned foods may be recommended for puppies with special dietary needs or for those who are underweight.

Disadvantages: Canned foods are high in fat and also high in water—about 78% of a can of food is moisture. Puppies have to eat more to get the nutrition they need, which can lead to obesity. Canned foods usually cost more than dry kibble, and the soft, pasty texture can lead to dental disease.

Semi-Moist Food

Advantage: Puppies usually like the taste.

Digest This

When looking for quality in your puppy's food, look for *digestible* ingredients. If ingredients are not easily digestible, your puppy won't be absorbing nutrients from them. Here is a list of ingredients, in order of digestibility:

- egg
- muscle meats (lamb, chicken, beef)
- organ meats (liver, kidney, heart)
- milk, cheese
- fish
- soy
- rice
- oats
- wheat
- corn

Disadvantages: To make it attractive to consumers (and dogs), semi-moist foods are usually high in sugar and salt. However, it can lead to dental disease.

Noncommercial Diets

Products made by dog food companies are not the only choice available. Homemade diets are gaining in popularity.

Home-Cooked Meals

You may prefer to cook your puppy's meals for yourself. If you do, consult your veterinarian and research how to create nutritionally complete meals for your puppy. Books and other resources are available, so study them for recipes. Don't just feed her what you eat. She's a different species, and she has different nutritional requirements.

The advantage to a home-cooked meal is that you can better control what goes into your puppy because you control all the ingredients. Keep in mind, though, that feeding a puppy table scraps is a leading cause of pancreatitis and obesity in dogs. Some foods that humans eat are also poisonous to dogs. In addition, cooked bones can splinter and injure your puppy's esophagus or digestive tract. So if you choose to prepare your puppy's meals, research exactly what to feed her.

Raw Diet

Raw or *biologically appropriate raw food* (BARF) diets are gaining in popularity. Advocates for the diet say that it more closely matches a puppy's nutritional needs and can help to prevent or cure certain diseases. They especially note that chewing on raw bones helps to clean a puppy's teeth and can

Dry food may assist in scraping plaque and tartar off the teeth.

help to prevent the dental issues that plague dogs as they get older. Opponents of the raw diet worry about the risk of salmonella poisoning, or they believe that raw bones can injure or even kill a dog.

Before trying a raw diet, do your research first. Some excellent books are available that outline how to safely feed a raw diet, so read them for recipes. If the thought of finding the time to prepare a raw diet seems daunting, some companies provide prepackaged raw diets that you can purchase.

Treats

Treats are great for training your puppy, and a wide variety of healthy treats are on the market from which to choose. You also can use hot dogs, string cheese, oat cereal, turkey, and other "people" food. These types of food are healthy because you're only going to use small amounts.

If your puppy has a food allergy, please consult your veterinarian before choosing a treat. If she is a small breed or has certain medical conditions, be careful of low-fat "people" food such as low-fat hot dogs or cheese. Some manufacturers take out the fat but add a lot of salt, which is not healthy. In general, treats should be:

- **Small and easy to swallow.** A treat shouldn't be a meal but a tiny bite.
- **Something that your puppy does not get every day.** Everyday kibble can quickly become boring. You need something that's different so that it cuts through the distractions.
- **Something that has an appealing odor to your puppy.** Your puppy can smell things you can't, which just increases the distractions she faces. She can smell someone grilling hamburgers down the block. If you use dry treats that don't have much odor, these treats will have a hard time cutting through the other odors that capture your puppy's interest. Use treats that your puppy can easily smell and discern as delicious.

Supplements

Only give your puppy a supplement if your veterinarian recommends it. If you are feeding your puppy a quality food that already has her daily nutritional requirements, you could be risking her health if you give her too much of a specific vitamin or mineral.

Ingredients to Avoid

Avoid flavorings and sugars because these are usually added to improve the taste of poorer-quality foods. Avoid colorings as well, which are usually added to make the food look better to owners. Also, avoid synthetic preservatives, such as BHA, BHT, and ethoxyquin. They are suspected to cause illness and disease in dogs, although nothing to date has been proven. The Federal Drug Administration's Center for Veterinary Medicine has asked dog food manufacturers to voluntary reduce the maximum amount of ethoxyquin in their foods while it is under study. Rather than take a chance, choose a food with a natural preservative, such as tocopherols or vitamin C.

Treats are great for training your puppy.

SETTING UP A FEEDING SCHEDULE

Scheduled feedings are better than *free feeding*, a method in which you leave the food bowl down all day and just fill it up as it empties. By setting up a feeding schedule for your puppy, you will better control what she consumes. Housetraining will be made easier as well, because puppies who are fed on a schedule will have to eliminate about the same time every day. If you leave food down for your puppy all day, she'll have to poop all day, too. Scheduled feedings also help to prevent obesity by controlling the amount of food a dog consumes.

Puppies younger than six months of age should get three meals a day. Puppies and adult dogs older than six months should get two meals a day.

To train your puppy to eat on a schedule, fill her bowl and put it down for ten minutes. After ten minutes, pick it back up (unless your puppy has already inhaled it!). If food remains in the bowl, that's okay. This will train her to eat when you give her food, not pick at it for hours on end. Don't worry, your puppy is smart. She won't starve. Just be consistent, and she'll learn.

TOXIC FOODS

Here is a partial list of foods that are dangerous or toxic to dogs. Never feed your dog these items, and make sure that you store or dispose of these items safely. For more information, please visit the

To help to prevent obesity, make sure that your puppy receives enough exercise.

National Animal Poison Control Center at www.aspca.org/apcc.

- alcoholic beverages
- avocado
- chives
- chocolate (all forms)
- coffee (all forms)
- fatty foods
- garlic
- macadamia nuts
- moldy or spoiled foods
- onions, onion powder
- products sweetened with xylitol
- raisins and grapes
- salt
- some mushrooms
- yeast dough

KEEPING A HEALTHY WEIGHT

Puppies are adorable when they're roly poly, but it isn't healthy for them to stay that way. Obesity is a leading cause of health problems among people in the United States, and our dogs are unfortunately following in our path.

How can you tell if your puppy is at her ideal weight? Use your hands. Put your hands on her shoulders, on either side of her body. Run them down along her sides toward her rear. You should be able to easily feel her ribs. (Don't squeeze, though!) If you can't easily feel her ribs, your puppy is overweight.

Obesity can cause a variety of serious health problems for your puppy. It could lead to diabetes, heart disease, increased blood pressure, decreased liver function, cancer, and damage to joints, bones, and ligaments. It could reduce her stamina, make her more prone to heatstroke, and make it difficult for her to breathe, which will be even worse if she is a flat-faced breed, such as a Pekinese. If you have a puppy with a long back, such as a Dachshund or Corgi, being overweight puts serious strain on her spine. The bottom line is that your puppy won't live as long if she's overweight.

You may not be able to prevent all the health scares that may come up during your puppy's life, but you *can* prevent obesity. Initially, feed your puppy using your chosen dog food's label recommendations, but always use your hands to check your puppy regularly to see if she's maintaining a proper weight. The food label's recommendations may be too much for your dog. Puppies also experience changes in their caloric requirements depending on their age and on how active they are. So the amount that you're feeding now will likely change several times as your dog matures. Keep her at a healthy weight so that you can enjoy her companionship for years to come.

By setting up a feeding schedule for your puppy, you will better control what she consumes.

How long should you feed puppy food before switching to adult? Opinions differ. Some recommend feeding puppy food until a puppy reaches physical maturity. Others recommend puppy food only for the first few months. Still others only recommend adult food for certain breeds, especially large or giant breeds. Talk with your breeder and veterinarian. Research respected sources. And most of all, keep a close eye on your puppy's health. If she's not eating well, her body and behavior can offer you clues that something's wrong.

4

GROOMING

Your Puppy

our puppy is gorgeous! Help her to stay that way with good grooming. It's never too early to start positive associations with your grooming supplies and procedures.

COAT CARE

What type of puppy you have will determine her grooming needs. For example, a Poodle puppy requires a great deal more grooming than a hairless Chinese Crested puppy. For advice about your specific puppy, consult her breeder or a professional groomer.

Brushing

No matter what kind of coat your puppy has, brush her on a regular basis. It will help to stimulate her skin, remove dead hair, and reduce shedding. The more fur you take off with a brush, the less will be on your floor, furniture, and clothing. You'll also help to prevent mats and tangles, which can be difficult to break up and can cause her to be afraid of you if you have to hurt her to get them out. Mats also can cause health problems if they are large or allowed to accumulate; the skin underneath them can become sore or infected.

How to Brush Your Puppy

If your puppy has never been exposed to a brush before, it may be startling to her. Or she may think that you're trying to play a game with her, and she may try to chew the brush. Don't get frustrated. You just need to teach her that brushing is a positive experience and that she needs to hold still while you are grooming her.

STEP 1:

a) Start by letting her sniff the brush, but don't let her chew on it. If necessary, spray it with a chew-deterrent spray.

Brush your puppy on a regular basis no matter what kind of coat she has.

b) It will be helpful if you have someone else to help you during these first few lessons. Your helper should feed your puppy treats while you introduce her to the brush. If it's just you, use one hand to feed an occasional treat and use the other hand to hold the brush. Take your time.

c) Pet your puppy and feed her a treat while you gently stroke her with the brush. Just do a few strokes, then stop.

STEP 2:

a) Repeat until she's comfortable being brushed.

b) If she is too wiggly, tire her out before attempting another session. It may help to wait until she's sleepy and more likely to be still.

Taking your time and making sure that your puppy enjoys her grooming sessions is better than forcing her down and frightening her. You're going to be brushing her for years to come, so teach her good grooming habits early.

Bathing

Puppies usually don't need baths as often as people want to give them. In fact, shampooing a puppy too frequently can lead to skin problems. A puppy's coat has oils in it that protect both the hair and the skin under it. If you strip those oils with frequent shampooing, you can cause your puppy's skin to become dry, which also can lead to infections. Some people find their puppies scratching all the time but can't find a flea on them. Washing your puppy too frequently may be the culprit. Talk to your breeder or a professional groomer about how often to bathe your puppy.

How to Bathe Your Puppy

Bathing your puppy shouldn't be a struggle or battle of wills. You can train your puppy to love bath time. First, get prepared:

1. Give your puppy a potty break.
2. Wear comfortable clothes that you don't mind getting wet.
3. Choose a good location, preferably a room where you can close the door in case she hops out of the tub. Remove any items that

you don't want to get wet in case your puppy shakes water everywhere.

4. Get all your supplies ready at hand. You don't want to leave your puppy unattended while you go find a towel. Also, get a supply of treats; you'll use these to associate the bath with a pleasant reward.

5. Brush her thoroughly and remove all mats and tangles. Getting them wet will make them worse.

6. Put a drop of mineral oil in each eye to prevent irritation from shampoo. Place cotton balls in her ears to prevent soap and water from getting in, but don't push them down into the ear canal.

Bath Time Tip

What if your puppy is trembling and afraid in the tub? It may be best to gradually work up to an entire bath rather than scaring her with the entire procedure. If your puppy is not taking treats, she is stressed. Break down your training into smaller steps. For example, just work on putting her in and out of the tub until she's comfortable with that step. Your goal is shorter, more positive training sessions.

STEP 1:

a) Put your puppy in the sink or bathtub. Give her a treat.

b) Gently start the water and let her get used to the sound. Give her a treat. Make sure that the water is warm but not too hot.

c) Get one leg wet. Give her a treat.

d) Get another leg wet. Give her a treat.

e) Gradually work up to wetting the entire puppy, treating as you go.

STEP 2:

a) Apply shampoo to her head, avoiding her eyes. Give her a treat.

b) Work backward toward her rear. Give her a treat.

c) Gradually work up to soaping the entire puppy, treating as you go. Talk to her throughout, and praise her for good behavior.

STEP 3:

a) Rinse thoroughly, making sure that you get all the shampoo out. Treat as you go.

b) Use a towel to dry her as much as possible. Don't forget to take out the cotton balls if you used them.

When you take your puppy out of the tub and put her down, immediately put on her collar and leash and take her out for a potty break. Puppies often have to pee after a bath. It's also normal if your puppy tears around your house like a maniac, rubbing against couch or bed pillows.

After your puppy's bath, dry her thoroughly.

EAR CARE

Check your puppy's ears regularly to make sure that they are not dirty and that no infection is present, especially if you have a drop-eared puppy. A small amount of brown, waxy substance is normal. If you see excessive wax in the ear canals or the ears have a discharge or smell bad, contact your veterinarian. Your puppy may have a bacterial or yeast infection, and she may need medication.

How to Clean Your Puppy's Ears

To clean your puppy's ears, get an ear cleanser from your veterinarian or pet supply store. Do not use alcohol because it is too harsh and could be painful. Dampen a cotton ball or cloth with ear cleanser, and gently wipe the inside of the ear flaps. Don't insert cotton-tipped swabs into the ear canal, or you could push bacteria and debris farther down into the ear canal. This can cause an infection.

EYE CARE

Tear stains are a common grooming issue, especially with little breeds and light-colored puppies. You may notice a brown or pinkish stain under your puppy's eyes. If it is excessive, talk to your veterinarian because there may be a problem with your puppy's tear ducts.

How to Clean Your Puppy's Eye Area

An accumulation of stains can lead to irritation and infection, so keep the area clean. You can purchase tear stain removal products from your veterinarian or pet supply store, but be careful not to get them in your puppy's eyes. Dampen a cotton ball or cloth with the solution and gently apply. If you've let the stains accumulate, it may take several cleanings to clear them up.

Keep your puppy's eye area clean with a soft cloth or cotton ball.

NAIL AND PAW CARE

Unless your puppy walks often on hard, abrasive surfaces, she will need her nails trimmed on a regular basis. Does the thought make you cringe? There's no need to be afraid. You can do it! You can even teach your puppy to enjoy the experience. It just takes some training for the both of you.

How to Care for Your Puppy's Nails

First, choose your equipment. Then, get your veterinarian, professional groomer, or a dog trainer to show you how to properly trim your puppy's nails. It may help you to see the process in action. In general, you first want to see if you can locate the "quick," which is the blood vessel. If your puppy has white nails, the quick is easy to find—it's the dark pink area. If your puppy has black nails, you won't be able to see the quick, so you'll just have to be more careful.

If you use a nail clipper, cut from below the paw, with the cutting edge of the clipper toward the end of the nail. Cut below the quick at a 45-degree angle. For puppies with black nails, the quick is the black dot that appears near the center of the nail where you trimmed it.

If you use a nail grinder, follow the directions that came with your tool. Be sure to hold the grinder to the nail for just a few seconds or the heat from the sander could be painful for your puppy.

Nail Trimming Tip

What if you're having trouble trimming your puppy's nails because she is simply too wiggly? Exercise her first to get her tired. It also may help to have someone else give her the treat while you practice doing her nails.

How to Care for Your Puppy's Paws

If your puppy has furry paws, trim the fur between her paw pads. Otherwise, she will have difficulty getting traction to walk properly, and the fur could attract dirt and debris that could cause injury or infections. The fur also could force her paw pads to spread apart, which could eventually cause hip or knee problems. Use blunt-tipped scissors or a small electric fur trimmer to gently trim the fur close to the paw pad.

Trim paw hair with scissors or an electric fur trimmer.

Training Your Puppy to Enjoy Nail and Paw Care

Now it's time to teach your puppy to enjoy her pedicure.

STEP 1:

a) Get a large spoon and a jar of peanut butter. Put a big glop of peanut butter on the spoon and give it to your puppy so that it coats the roof of her mouth.

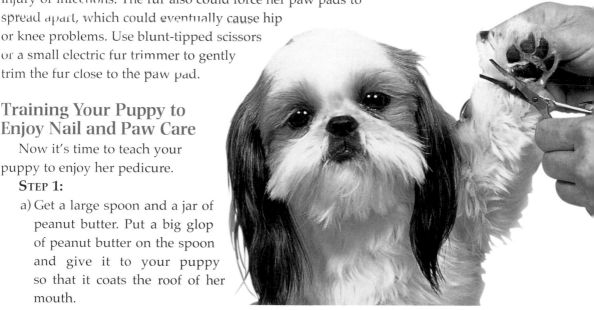

b) While she's licking the peanut butter, show her the clippers. If you're using a grinding tool, turn it on for a few seconds and then shut it off.

c) Quit for the day.

d) Repeat for one week until your puppy is very happy at the sight of the clippers or grinder.

STEP 2:

a) Give your puppy the peanut butter.

b) While she's licking, gently touch the clippers or grinder to one nail.

c) Quit for the day.

d) The next night, touch two nails. Quit.

e) Repeat until you can touch all nails.

STEP 3:

a) Give your puppy the peanut butter.

b) While she's licking, cut one nail.

c) Quit for the day.

d) Over the course of several days, gradually work up to cutting all nails.

STEP 4:

a) Repeat these steps for trimming paw hair using your scissors or electric fur trimmer. Gradually work up to where your puppy is comfortable having her paws trimmed.

There's no law that says you have to cut all nails or trim all paws at once. Puppies learn best in gradual doses. If you make the process pleasant for your dog throughout, she'll learn that there's nothing to be afraid of—and you will, too.

Nail Grinding Tip

If you use a nail grinder to keep your puppy's nails short, try slipping a nylon knee-high stocking over her foot before grinding. Pull it snugly so that her nails pop out through the stocking but her fur is kept wrapped tight against her body. This will prevent the grinder from catching on her fur and causing injury.

DENTAL CARE

With all that your puppy is chewing on right now, the last thing you're probably thinking about is dental care. But over time, plaque and tartar will build up on those pearly whites, which could lead to periodontal disease. This is a very painful condition that may lead to tooth loss and jawbone damage, as well as cause disorders in your dog's heart, liver, and kidneys.

To help prevent periodontal disease, your veterinarian may recommend periodic dental cleanings for your dog, which will require anesthesia. You can save yourself some veterinary bills and bad dog breath by simply brushing your puppy's teeth several times a week. This should decrease (but not eliminate) the need for professional cleanings.

Before you begin, get your puppy used to you handling her mouth. You can put some peanut butter on your finger and let her lick it off. While she's licking, run your fingers along her gum line. Repeat this a few times until she's comfortable with you handling her mouth.

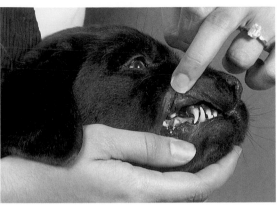

How to Brush Your Puppy's Teeth

Always use a pet toothpaste, not your own. Human toothpaste may upset your puppy's stomach. You can choose a puppy toothbrush, sponge, or pad to apply the toothpaste. Most puppies love the taste. If your puppy is wiggly or hesitant, gradually work up to brushing her teeth just as you did trimming her nails.

Inspect your dog's teeth as part of her regular grooming routine.

To brush your puppy's teeth, let her have a taste of the toothpaste at first. Then, brush her teeth using a circular motion, covering each tooth. You may want to start with just her front teeth and her canines (the large teeth in the front of the mouth) until you both get used to the routine. As she grows more comfortable, continue on to the back teeth.

Make tooth brushing a positive experience for your puppy. By taking care of her teeth now, you'll be helping her keep them well into her senior years.

ANAL SAC CARE

Does your puppy sit on the ground and drag her rear across the floor? This is called "scooting," and it's usually a sign that she has impacted anal sacs, or glands. This seems to happen more often with toy or small-breed puppies.

Dogs have anal sacs on either side of their anal openings at the 4 o'clock and 8 o'clock positions. These sacs have tiny ducts under the skin that lead to an opening right next to the anus. Every time your puppy passes a stool, it should press hard enough against the anal sac to cause it to express a foul-smelling secretion that deposits on the stool as it passes. This secretion lets other dogs know who your puppy is. That's also why dogs smell each other's rears when they greet each other.

Don't Forget the Dewclaws

Dewclaws are extra nails on the inside of a puppy's leg. Some puppies have dewclaws, while others have them removed a few days after birth. Some puppies only have them on the back legs, some have them in the front and back, and some breeds, like the Great Pyrenees, have double dewclaws. If your puppy has dewclaws, don't forget to trim them. They can grow into the soft tissue of her leg if left unclipped.

How to Care for Your Puppy's Anal Sacs

If your puppy's anal sacs get clogged or infected, she will feel discomfort. She'll scoot to try to relieve the pressure. If they abscess, your puppy will be in a lot of pain. If you suspect that her anal glands are abscessed, consult your veterinarian to see if she requires antibiotics. Your veterinarian also may suggest a diet change to one that's higher in fiber.

Your veterinarian or a professional groomer can show you how to express the anal sacs yourself so that you can save yourself a trip to the office or grooming parlor. It's not the most pleasant task, but you may find that your puppy needs regular anal sac expressing to remain in good health.

If your puppy is not scooting, it's best to leave her anal sacs alone. If you start expressing them when she doesn't need it, you may have to express them regularly in the future.

CHOOSING A PROFESSIONAL GROOMER

If you have a puppy who requires a lot of grooming or if you don't have the time or desire to do her grooming yourself, consider hiring a professional groomer. Grooming services include bathing, combing, brushing, cutting or shaving mats, trimming nails, cleaning ears, and helping to control external parasites such as fleas and ticks.

Here's how to narrow your search:

- Ask for recommendations from your veterinarian, dog trainer, and friends.
- Check with your Better Business Bureau to see if any complaints have been registered about the groomer.
- Ask if the groomer belongs to the National Dog Groomers Association of America, Inc. (NDGAA), an association that promotes professional grooming standards.
- Ask if the groomer offers references from other clients.

Once you've narrowed your list, it's time to tour your choices and meet the groomers in person. Here's what to look for in a quality groomer:

- Is the facility clean?
- Is the staff friendly and knowledgeable? What kind of training or certifications do they have? Are they gentle with the animals?

- Are the cages appropriately sized for the animals in them?
- Do they monitor pets regularly to prevent overheating from hair dryers?
- Do they keep complete pet records, including medical and emergency contact information?
- How do they deal with problem puppy behavior? For example, if your puppy is bouncing around on the grooming table, you don't want a staff member shaking her by the scruff of her neck. Do all staff members follow reward-based methods of training?
- What are the fees?

Once you have chosen a groomer, it's best to make your first visit a training one. A quality groomer will work with you to make your puppy's experience positive. Take her to the groomer and bring your treats. Ask the staff to give them to your puppy. Ask the groomer to handle your puppy, offering praise and treats throughout. If your dog is doing well, you also can introduce some of the grooming equipment to her. Let her smell it, and give her treats for being brave and curious. Then, bring her home. If you keep the session short and fun, she'll enjoy going there again. Also, practice your grooming and socializing exercises (explained in Chapter 5) so that your puppy will be more comfortable.

Helping the Nervous Puppy

What if your puppy is trembling or nervous during her grooming visit? Make several visits to get your puppy acquainted with the groomer, and keep each visit very short. Break everything down into smaller parts so that your puppy can acclimate better. Your goal is for her to have a good time, not be stressed. You may need to call a professional dog trainer if your puppy is very shy or fearful. You don't want her to be so afraid that she feels the need to lash out to protect herself.

Grooming your puppy is an important way to get her used to you handling her all over her body. You should be able to touch her anywhere without her becoming frightened or irritated. There may come a time when you have to treat her for an injury or administer medicine, and you want her to be comfortable with your touch. It's easier to teach that to a young puppy than to an older dog who isn't used to handling. Your veterinarian and groomer also will appreciate your efforts because your puppy will be easier for them to handle when they need to care for her.

Chapter

5

TRAINING
Your Puppy

The puppy you brought home is unlike any other dog you've ever owned. No two puppies are alike. Treat her like the precious individual she is, and have patience—with both of you—while you start your training program. It takes effort to train a puppy, and it's not going to magically happen overnight. It may be hard work, but the results are worth every effort. And if you use reward-based methods, you'll learn that just because it's work doesn't mean that it can't be fun.

WHY TRAINING IS IMPORTANT

Would you like a puppy who goes up to people and sits politely to be petted, rather than jumping all over them to get attention? Do you want a puppy who only pees and poops outside your home, rather than on your carpet? Do you want a puppy who doesn't chew your furniture to bits or destroy your household belongings? Wouldn't this be a great puppy to share your life with? Puppies aren't born knowing how to behave in that way, though—you have to teach them.

You want your puppy to learn manners so that she can fit into your family routine. You want her to respond to you when you ask her to do something, because doing so will help to keep her safe from harm. You can achieve these goals by training your puppy. Rather than getting frustrated with all the things she's doing wrong, teach her how to do things right.

It's never too early to start training your puppy. In fact, if you wait too long, you may end up with behavioral problems or bad habits that will be harder to fix later. Puppies are great sponges for learning.

There will be times in training when you will get frustrated and feel that you're just not getting through to your puppy. This is normal. Perhaps you've never taught a puppy before, so you're learning something new, too. Maybe you have trained a puppy before, but are trying these modern, reward-based methods for the first time. Or maybe you have fond memories of an older dog who never seemed to need training because he was perfect. If you

Communicating With Your Puppy

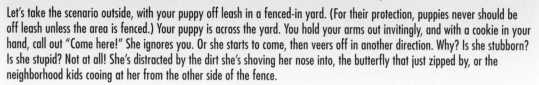

Your puppy doesn't have a clue to what you are saying. She doesn't understand when you call out "Fluffy, come here!" She has no idea what "Come here" means. She can learn, but you have to teach her. More importantly, you have to teach her in terms that she can understand. What seems very clear to you may not make a whole lot of sense to your puppy. Remember, she is a different species than you. Her brain is wired differently, so she learns differently.

If you ask your puppy to do something and she doesn't do it, is she stubborn? Is she defying you? Could it be that she's just not intelligent? Not likely. The truth is that she either doesn't understand what you're asking, or you have unrealistic expectations about her ability to perform the task. For example, let's say you're trying to teach your puppy to come to you when you call her. You're indoors, with the television turned off and no distractions. You crouch down, hold your arms open invitingly, treat in hand, and croon "Come here!" Your puppy runs to you, tail wagging happily. Does this mean that she understands the cue? Nope!

Let's take the scenario outside, with your puppy off leash in a fenced-in yard. (For their protection, puppies never should be off leash unless the area is fenced.) Your puppy is across the yard. You hold your arms out invitingly, and with a cookie in your hand, call out "Come here!" She ignores you. Or she starts to come, then veers off in another direction. Why? Is she stubborn? Is she stupid? Not at all! She's distracted by the dirt she's shoving her nose into, the butterfly that just zipped by, or the neighborhood kids cooing at her from the other side of the fence.

This is normal any time you change your puppy's immediate environment. If you teach her something with just you in the room but later try to get her to do the same thing with other people present, you may find that she has difficulty responding. That's because added distractions are competing for your puppy's attention. Now, this doesn't mean that your puppy will never learn to respond to you outside or with other people present. It just means that you have to have extra patience to teach her what you want.

did indeed have one of those dogs, consider yourself very lucky, because it rarely happens twice!

REWARDS FOR A REWARDING RELATIONSHIP

The techniques in this chapter use modern, reward-based methods of training based on scientifically proven results. More and more, puppy owners are discovering that, by training their puppies with positive methods, they get more positive results.

This wasn't always the case. Long ago, it was the standard to use punishment to train dogs. When training an exercise, an owner would watch his dog intently. The second she did something wrong, he would immediately yank her collar to cause her discomfort or pain. For some dogs, this did produce results; they learned to avoid punishment by only doing certain things. What became apparent over the years, however, was that this method of training also sometimes caused undesirable side effects, including shyness, aggression, and distrust of owners. Some dogs would just shut down because they were confused. They figured it was easier not to do anything than to try something that would risk punishment. Unfortunately, some owners mistook this helplessness as a good thing. A dog who held a 45-minute *down-stay* but who was afraid to move and miserable the entire time, was thought to be a well-behaved dog.

You don't have to settle for good behavior from an unhappy puppy. You can have both a happy puppy and a well-behaved puppy all rolled into one. It all depends on how you teach her.

Dog training has evolved a lot over the years. Today, we know that we can achieve results without resorting to using punishment. Think of the last time you learned something completely new. Did the person teaching you yell at you every time you got something wrong? Did he rap you on the knuckles? If so, you may have learned the task, but how did you feel during the instruction? Were you afraid to make a mistake? How did you feel about the teacher?

Perhaps you had a different experience. Did you have a teacher who showed you what to do and praised you when you did well? Did you earn extras in class, like chocolate or gift certificates? How did you feel during the instruction? Did you look forward to the class?

A food treat is one of the most enticing rewards that you can offer your puppy.

The difference is the training philosophy. You can either focus on what your puppy does wrong, or focus on what she does right. If you focus on good behavior and reward it, your puppy will perform those good behaviors again and again.

Advantages of Reward-Based Training

Reward-based methods don't just work with "easy" dogs—they work with all different breeds and different types of dog personalities. One great advantage is that you don't have to be physically stronger than your puppy to get her to

Disciplining Your Puppy

Using physical punishment to discipline your puppy can backfire. Some of the old-fashioned ways to punish a puppy include scruff shakes, the "alpha roll," and spanking. These actions easily teach your puppy to be afraid of your hands, which can create aggressive or shy puppies.

The best way to discipline your puppy is to train her to do what you want. Instead of getting frustrated at her for doing something wrong, teach her to do something right. If you do have a situation where you need to let your puppy know she did something wrong, use a stern voice only. If you use a pleasant voice to train and play with your puppy, and only use your "discipline voice" when she does something wrong, she will easily recognize when you are displeased. Wouldn't it be much easier to control your puppy with your voice rather than having to get physical?

do what you want. With old-fashioned training, whoever could muscle the dog into doing something got results. But what if your puppy is an exuberant 40-pound (18.1-kg) Golden Retriever mix? You want your puppy to work for all members of your family, not just those who are stronger than she is. What good is it if your puppy stops jumping on the adults but continues to leap on the kids? Reward-based training does not rely on brawn; it relies on brains. You don't out-muscle your puppy—you outsmart her!

Another great advantage of using reward-based methods is that it works very well with puppies who are shy or timid. If you try to train a scared puppy by punishing her every time she does something wrong while learning a task, you'll likely create a *really* scared puppy. This puppy may start lifting her lip or growling or snapping at you because she is afraid. She's trying to make the scary teacher go away. By using reward-based methods with a shy dog, you'll teach the puppy that learning is fun. She'll gain confidence the more she learns, and she'll be more likely to become bolder and less afraid of her environment and the people around her.

A common myth about reward-based training is that it's for permissive puppy parents and that, if you use positive methods, you'll end up with a puppy who walks all over you and thinks she's "the boss." This is not true. Just because you use positive methods doesn't make you a pushover! You can easily use rewards and still be the leader of your pack. You should still set up rules and a structure for your puppy to live by. If you use reward-based training methods, it's actually easier for you to be in charge because you'll control all the good things your puppy wants.

Tools for Training With Rewards

Food, praise, and life rewards are some of the most enticing treats that you can offer your puppy.

Food

Food charts the fastest course to your puppy's brain. Puppies are easily distracted, and they have no attention spans. Your puppy is likely to forget all those outside temptations if you pay her with a food reward.

Praise

Praise can be very motivating to a puppy. For some behaviors, you should praise exuberantly. For example, when your puppy comes to you, it's cause for celebration! Other times, it may be best to praise softly. For example, if you're trying to teach your puppy to lie down, using a soft, happy voice is a better idea. If you are too excited in your praise, your puppy may leap up out of the *down* position.

Life Rewards

Life rewards are anything that your puppy finds appealing: a game of fetch, a ride in the car, a belly rub, sniffing a mailbox. For example, if your puppy loves to play with other dogs, you can use this as a reward in your training. Before she gets to play with the other dog, ask her to sit first. Once she sits, release her to go play. She'll learn to sit faster, so that she gets to play faster.

Which Tool Is Best?

Every puppy is different. Some will melt for an ear scratch, while others just want you to hurry up and throw the ball. For others, a piece of hot dog trumps your sweet talk. It's important to get to know your puppy and her individual motivators. Also, keep in mind that motivators don't work the same way every time. Your puppy may eagerly come when called in your living room for a piece of kibble, but it may take a piece of prime rib to reward her for quitting a squirrel chase. Vary it so that she doesn't get bored.

SOCIALIZATION

One of the most valuable lessons you can teach your puppy is that the world is a safe place, with kind humans and friendly dogs and other animals. The act of exposing your puppy to the world is called *socialization*. Many puppy owners have heard that this is important but really don't know how to go about doing it correctly. If you do it right, you'll help your puppy grow up to be confident and outgoing. If it's done wrong, you can inadvertently create a frightened, aggressive puppy.

A critical time for your puppy's learning is from birth to 16 weeks of age. During this time, puppies can absorb a great deal of information, but they are also very vulnerable to bad experiences. Puppies who are not properly exposed to different types of people and other animals can find them very startling or frightening when they do finally encounter them at an older age. They may react by growling, cowering, or even biting. But if they have positive experiences with people and animals before they turn 16 weeks of age, they are less likely to be afraid of them later.

Soon after you bring your puppy home (preferably no younger than eight weeks of age), it's time to start your socialization training program.

Protecting Your Puppy's Health

Most puppies will not get all their shots until they are 15 to 16 weeks of age. Some breeders and veterinarians recommend an even more extended schedule. It's very important that you do not expose your puppy to dangerous diseases until she's had vaccinations to protect her.

Puppies can get diseases by walking where sick dogs have been and by picking up traces of feces or other bodily fluids. Some viruses, such as the parvovirus, are extremely durable and contagious, and it only takes a small amount of exposure to infect your puppy. How do you prevent exposure?

Do not let your puppy walk in public places. This means that you should not let your puppy walk in the neighborhood or in public parks until she has had all her shots. If you must take your puppy to these places, carry her. Of course, this will be easier with a Maltese puppy than it will be with an English Mastiff, but it's up to you to keep your puppy safe.

The need to keep your puppy safe from disease can compete with the need to socialize her. If the ideal window for socialization is up to 16 weeks, and your puppy will not complete her shot series before then, how can you expose her to the world? Here's how to do it safely:

- **Invite friends and family to your house.** If your puppy can't

Socialize your puppy to calm, friendly children.

get out, bring the people in! Ask them to remove their shoes before coming into your home just in case they've stepped in something that can cause your puppy harm.

- **Invite safe, friendly dogs to your home.** If you have friends who have suitable dogs for your puppy to meet, invite them to come play at your place.
- **Only visit safe houses.** If you have friends who have a suitable, healthy dog who would play well with your puppy, visit their homes. This is safer than letting your puppy walk in a public park or in a neighborhood where you don't know the dogs who have been there. Be sure to carry your puppy from the car into your friend's home.
- **Do not let your puppy run up to dogs you don't know, especially at the veterinarian's office.** Dogs who visit the veterinarian may be sick. If you let your puppy greet them, you could be exposing her to a contagious disease. Carry your young puppy into the veterinarian's office, and keep her in your lap (or in her crate) until her immune system is protected.

These simple steps will allow you to socialize your puppy while minimizing exposure to disease.

Socialization to People

Here are some guidelines for positive socialization experiences with people:

- **Pick different people.** Puppies should be exposed to people of different genders, different ethnicities, different ages, different shapes and sizes. The more variety you introduce, the quicker she will learn that variety is the spice of life!
- **Pick the right people.** Make sure that everyone you choose to interact with your puppy knows how to do so in a positive manner. If children cannot hold or pet your puppy correctly, they should not interact with her. If an adult will be rough with your puppy, he should not interact with her. Remember, a negative experience during this critical time can make your puppy afraid.

Once you have the right people in place, here are some fun socialization games to play.

Pass the Puppy

Divide your puppy's meal of kibble into small plastic bags, one bag for each person visiting. Before starting the game, if necessary explain to everyone how to properly hold the puppy by supporting her rear end. The first person then picks up the puppy and gives her a piece of kibble. The person touches one of her paws, gives

Puppies should be exposed to people of different genders, different ethnicities, and of different shapes and sizes.

her a piece of kibble. Touches another paw, gives a piece of kibble. Touches her ears, gives a piece of kibble. Touches her tail, gives a piece of kibble. Looks at her teeth, gives a piece of kibble. Then the person passes the puppy on to the next person, who goes through the same routine. This game teaches your puppy that it's rewarding to have people touch her all over her body.

Puppy Recalls

Divide your puppy's meal of kibble into small plastic bags, one bag for each person visiting. Have everyone sit in a circle on the floor, with the puppy in the center of the circle. One person calls the puppy to come and holds out the piece of kibble. When the puppy goes to the person, she gets the kibble and lots of petting and praising. Then someone else in the circle repeats the routine. This game teaches your puppy that it's rewarding to approach people.

Socialization to Other Dogs

If your puppy will ever be around other dogs, whether it's in the neighborhood, in a future training class, or with future dogs you have at home, it's important to expose her to different dogs at an early age so that she learns to get along with them properly. Puppies who are not socialized with other dogs sometimes never learn to "speak dog" and have fear or aggression problems with members of their own species.

It's very important to only pick safe dogs to interact with your puppy so that she has positive experiences. If you have a tiny 3-pound (1 4-kg) Yorkshire Terrier, it's not a good idea to let her play with a bouncy 30-pound (13.6-kg) Labrador Retriever puppy. The Lab puppy could hurt your Yorkie without meaning to; the size difference is just too great. Now, if it's an older Labrador Retriever with a proven history of being safe and gentle around young puppies, it may be perfectly fine. Just be sure that you know the other dog well before risking injury.

Socialization: What Not to Do

All socialization is not good socialization. Bad experiences at an early age can make negative impressions for years to come. Sometimes, certain situations are just too much for your puppy. If she is having a good time, she will look the part. Her ears will be

Expose your puppy to other dogs at an early age so that she learns to get along with them properly.

up, her eyes will be bright, and she may wag her tail or whole body and actively seek interaction.

If your puppy is not enjoying herself, learn to recognize her signs of stress to avoid causing emotional harm:

- cowering or clinging
- ears down and back
- lip licking
- sleeping (all young puppies take frequent naps, but if you find your puppy sleeping a lot when you have her out or at a busy event, she may actually be shutting down)
- tail tucking
- turning the head or body away from people who approach
- yawning

For example, let's say you take your puppy to your child's soccer game. You see that she's flinching at the loudspeaker and getting a bit clingy. She starts to whine. Your child's team rushes around her to pet her. She licks her lips, turns her head away, and yawns. She tries to crawl in your lap or under the bleachers. These signs of stress mean that your puppy is not having a good socialization experience. You may actually be teaching her that children, large groups of people, or playing fields are cause for worry. Forcing her to remain there or hoping she'll get used to it might only make things worse. If you see signs of stress in your puppy, immediately remove her from the situation until she relaxes.

Take it much slower with your puppy, and gradually get her used to this level of stimulation.

CRATE TRAINING

Crate training is the act of teaching your puppy to enter her enclosure and enjoy spending time in it. If you properly introduce the crate and train your puppy to enjoy confinement, she'll consider it her safe den. If you simply put her in the crate without making it a positive experience, she could grow fearful of it or begin to dislike it. Crate train your puppy so that both of you can make the most of this useful tool.

Begin crate training the very first night you bring your puppy home. If you let her sleep on your bed the first few nights, and then realize that it's not a good idea because she's peeing on the bedspread, she will have a harder time understanding why you're suddenly asking her to sleep in her crate.

Where to Put the Crate

First, decide where you want to keep her crate. It should be in a place where your family gathers regularly, rather than isolated by itself. Some puppy parents choose to get two crates—one for the family's common area and one for a bedroom—so that they don't have to move the crate at bedtime. Whether to let your puppy sleep in your bedroom is a personal choice. Most puppies would prefer to be near you, but if you don't like the idea, that's fine. But start with one plan and stick to it, or you'll confuse your puppy.

Vary the toys that your puppy has in her crate.

What to Put in the Crate

The following are some items to consider putting in your puppy's crate.

Bedding

Be very careful before putting bedding in your dog's crate. If she chews or shreds a blanket or dog bed, she could swallow pieces and cause a stomach obstruction. Your puppy will be fine without bedding and can earn the right to have it later, once she's less prone to destructive behavior.

Food and Water

It's fine to feed your puppy in her crate. Per her feeding schedule, put the food in her crate for about ten 10 minutes and then remove it. You don't want to leave food for her all day or she'll have to poop all day.

Some puppies do fine with water in their crates, while others prefer to splash it everywhere. Some crates come with plastic bowls that attach to the crate door. If your puppy chews the plastic, try a metal coop cup instead. If she still makes a wet mess, don't leave water in her crate. Make sure that you're following a realistic crate schedule for your puppy and that she gets plenty of fresh water when outside the crate each day.

Toys

Your puppy will love having toys in her crate. Be sure that they are safe for unsupervised chewing.

Crate Training: The Basics

Pick a short cue to teach your puppy that you want her to enter her crate. It can be "Go to kennel!" or "Kennel up!" or even "Go to jail!" It doesn't matter what words you use—just be sure that you and everyone in your family use the same cue each time.

STEP 1:

a) Have the crate door open. Get some delicious treats that your puppy likes. You can even use her kibble breakfast for this exercise.

b) Show your puppy a treat, and toss or place it in the crate. You may find that you need to put the treats near the crate door at first. You can even leave a little trail of treats from the crate door toward the back of the crate. Don't shut the door behind her yet.

c) When your puppy goes in after the treat, praise her.

d) Repeat this exercise several times over the course of a few hours.

Common Challenges:

- Remember, puppies have no attention spans. If you toss a treat in the crate, and she hears a noise outside that distracts her, she'll forget there ever was a treat. You'll have to remind her.

- If she's not interested at all, try using different treats. Space the exercise out more so that you're not overwhelming her.

STEP 2:

a) Pick up your puppy. Give your cue "Go to kennel!" or whatever cue you chose, and gently place your puppy in her crate.

b) Immediately give her a treat and praise her.

c) Shut the crate door for a few seconds. Talk cheerfully to your puppy.

No Collars in Crates

Remove your puppy's collar when she's in her crate. It can get caught in the wire and cause a choking hazard.

  - Try not to say things like "It's okay, you poor thing in jail, it's okay, I'll let you out soon," because you're really teaching your puppy that things are not okay. Don't reassure her as if something was wrong. Just happily tell her she's a good girl for being in her crate.
  - If your puppy paws at the crate door or cries, whines, or barks, completely ignore her. Don't talk to her, and don't even look at her. If you do, you'll just reward that behavior. Just wait until she calms down. Only pay attention to her when she's behaving the way you want.

d) When your puppy is calm, open the crate door. Do it very casually, without excitement. If you make a big deal when your puppy *leaves* the crate, you're teaching her that getting out is a good thing. You want to teach her to get *in* the crate instead!

e) Repeat this a couple times, gradually increasing the amount of time that your puppy is in her crate, going from a few seconds to a few minutes.

Tips:

- Use your cue every time you put your puppy in her crate. Give her a treat each time, too.
- Be sure that your puppy gets plenty of playtime, affection, and potty breaks outside the crate.

STEP 3:

After a few days of crate routine, it's time to teach your puppy to go into her crate on her own, rather than you placing her there.

a) Get a treat in your hand. Show it to your puppy, and give her the cue "Go to kennel!" Then use the treat in your hand to lure her into the crate. If she follows it in, give it to her when she gets into the crate and praise her. Repeat several times a day. If she does not follow the treat lure into the crate, try using more tempting treats.

Crating When You're Home

If you only crate your puppy when you leave the house, she may begin to associate her crate with you leaving, which may cause her to dislike her den. To prevent this, train your puppy that she may sometimes need to be crated when you're at home.

Crate Training: Next Steps

Because of your work schedule, you may need to leave your puppy during the day for long periods of time soon after you bring her home. This can be unavoidable. Just be sure that you are keeping to a realistic schedule.

You can still teach your puppy to enjoy confinement for longer periods of time. Start this training after she is readily going into her crate when you give her the cue.

STEP 1:

a) Cue your puppy with "Go to kennel!" Give her a food-stuffed rubber toy and praise her when she enters the crate. Shut the crate door, then leave the room or just go about the house as you normally would.

b) Wait a few minutes, then walk by her crate. If she is behaving and not whining, pawing at the crate door, or barking, praise her and give her a treat through the crate door. If she is acting up, ignore her and walk past.

STEP 2:

a) Repeat, gradually working up to longer periods of time in between treats. You're teaching your puppy that good things happen when she's in her crate.

b) After about ten minutes, if your puppy is calm, open the crate door. Be relaxed and don't praise her for getting out of the crate.

STEP 3:

a) Gradually work up to longer periods inside the crate.

Tips:

• The longer she's in her crate, the better the treats should get. Start with regular kibble, then work up to liver or other tasty treats. Your puppy will learn that the longer she's in her crate, the better it gets.

• Vary her toys. If you only give her a food-stuffed toy in her crate when you leave, she could start associating that toy with you leaving and may not like it anymore.

Once your puppy is happily running into her crate when you give the cue, and staying there for longer periods of time, you are ready for these next steps:

STEP 4:

a) You are going to stop using a treat to lure your puppy

into her crate. Stand by the crate and give the cue "Go to kennel!" Point inside the crate as if you have a treat in your hand. This is not to trick your puppy. Her nose tells her it's not there. Instead, you are using the same hand signal that you've actually been teaching her all along. Dogs learn body language much faster than verbal language, so if you use your hands the same way, she will better understand what you want of her.

It's fine to put water in your puppy's crate, as long as she doesn't chew on the bowl or decide to go swimming.

b) As soon as she goes into the crate, praise her. Shut the door, quickly get a treat from where you keep them, and give it to her through the crate door. This will teach your puppy that you may not always have treats with you, but she should still do what you ask because she'll be rewarded.

STEP 5:

a) Gradually move farther and farther away from the crate as you give your cue "Go to kennel."

When Can My Puppy Have More Freedom?

It may seem that your young puppy spends a lot of time in her crate, so it's very important that you give her plenty of exercise and affection outside the crate each day. Don't use the crate as a crutch. Your puppy needs supervised time with you outside her crate, especially if you have an active breed.

After your puppy has done well in her crate for a while, you may be tempted to give her more freedom in the house unsupervised. If this happens too soon, though, you will find that you've made a serious mistake. Puppies can be destructive chewers into adulthood—depending on your puppy's breed, that could be a couple of years. If you let an adolescent puppy loose in your home,

Two Time's the Charm

Say you take your puppy out once, and she pees and poops. Then you bring her inside, and she does it again right there on the floor. Why is she going again? Don't worry—this is normal. Young puppies often have to pee and poop twice in one outing, so give your dog time to eliminate twice outside.

especially at about eight to nine months, when her back molars are coming in and she has a great need to chew, she could make quite a mess. More importantly, she could chew or eat something that will hurt her. So how do you know she's ready?

1. Your puppy should be completely done with her chewing stage. This means that she has not chewed something inappropriately for a couple months.

2. Your puppy should be completely housetrained, meaning that she has not peed or pooped in the house—at all—in a couple months.

This combination usually does not happen until your puppy is an adult dog. You must wait until she's achieved these goals, or you will undo all your hard work.

HOUSETRAINING

Housetraining is one of the most common complaints of new puppy owners. It can be very frustrating to find puddles on your carpet or poop under the dining room table. The most common problem with housetraining actually boils down to communication.

1. **Puppies don't have a clue that you want them to eliminate outside.** They are not born knowing that they shouldn't pee or poop on your carpet or floors. Also, puppies don't understand human language, so you need to teach them in terms that they can understand.

2. **Most puppies will *not* give you a signal when they need to eliminate.** In fact, many people are surprised that their puppies do not run to the door or bark or paw at it when they have to potty. (If you do have one of these puppies, you're lucky!) If you want your puppy to give you a signal, you have to train her to do so.

3. **Using multiple methods of housetraining will confuse your puppy.** For example, don't use newspapers or potty pads and ask your puppy to also eliminate outside. With all these choices, how is she supposed to learn? I do not recommend using indoor training methods to housetrain puppies because it teaches them that it's okay to eliminate in the home.

Housetraining: The Basics

This book's goal for housetraining is to teach your dog to

eliminate outside and only outside. It's best to start this program the day you bring your puppy home. The more accidents your puppy has indoors, the more she is practicing eliminating in your home. The longer you wait, the harder it will be to change this habit as your puppy grows into an adult. You want her to practice eliminating *outside* your home so that this becomes her habit instead.

Your first steps are to set up a feeding schedule and realistic daily schedule for your puppy. Try hard to keep to this schedule every day. Dogs respond well to routines. You may soon learn that your puppy tries to keep you on schedule! The more that you can stick to a daily routine, the faster your puppy will learn housetraining.

In general, puppies need a potty break when they wake up (even from a nap), after they eat, after they play, and after a bath. They also need a potty break after the "zoomies"—when their eyes glaze over and they run around like crazy animals. (That's a typical puppy behavior. They usually outgrow it, but it can be startling the first time you see it!)

Puppies cannot hold their bladder and bowels all day. They must have a lunchtime potty break. This can be difficult if you work outside the home, but it's part of having a puppy in your life. It won't be forever, just for about the first six months. Don't be fooled if your young puppy manages to "hold it" for longer periods of time. These puppies can be prone to developing urinary tract or kidney infections. Don't take the chance! Also, don't skip the midday break and just accept that your puppy will soil her crate (or the floor, if you're not using a crate). This will teach her that it's okay to eliminate indoors, and it will take much longer to break this habit.

Either hire a pet sitter, get a neighbor or friend to come over, or arrange to come home at lunch for the first six months. You will have a much better chance of successfully housetraining your puppy for the rest of her life.

There are nine potty breaks in the sample schedule on page 81. That gives you nine chances each day to teach your puppy to eliminate outside. Of course, if you have a family member at home, you won't need to enlist your neighbor's help for the midday break.

When you're creating your schedule, factor in your dog's type,

Help Her Succeed

If you can't watch your puppy, she must be confined so that she doesn't have the opportunity to eliminate in the house. For example, it's not fair to let your puppy have the run of your bedroom at night if she's not housetrained, then get mad at her for having an accident during the night. Crate her overnight until she's completely housetrained. Then she can earn more freedom.

Signs that your puppy has to eliminate may include sniffing or circling.

age, and activities. Toy breeds do seem to need more potty breaks than do larger puppies. Also, the younger the puppy, the more potty breaks you should take. If your puppy is very playful and active, she may need more potty breaks as well.

Housetraining: Next Steps

Now that you've set up everything for a successful housetraining program, it's time to actually train your puppy to eliminate outside.

STEP 1:

a.) Attach a leash to your puppy. Puppies are easily distracted; one second your dog will start to pee, and the next she'll catch a scent of something and dash off. If you are attached to your puppy, you can help to minimize distractions.

b.) Hide a couple small treats in your hand. Get ready to reward your puppy immediately for eliminating outside.

STEP 2:

a.) Take your puppy outside. If you want, you can give this a cue, such as "Wanna go outside?" If you use the same cue every time with the same action, your puppy will learn to associate the two.

b.) Watch your puppy for signs that she has to eliminate, such as sniffing the ground or assuming the position to go. As soon as she starts, give her your cue to potty, such as "Go potty" or "Do your business." Make sure that you and your family use the same cue every time. Consistency is important.

c.) Give a set amount of time for your puppy to find the right spot. If you want her to potty within five minutes, you can teach her to do that. Give her only five minutes. If she hasn't gone, bring her back inside and crate her for 15 minutes, then try again. Be consistent. Don't give your puppy 30 minutes to eliminate on the weekend and then get frustrated when she takes 30 minutes Monday morning.

d.) When she's done peeing, give her the treat and praise her. Don't wait for her to both pee and poop. Reward her for each action.

Step 3:

a.) If you want your puppy to now play in her fenced yard, take off her leash and give her another cue, such as "Go play!" By making sure that she potties first, you'll teach her to get it out of the way before her playtime. This will be convenient when

Sample Schedule

Here is a sample housetraining schedule for a typical family that is gone during the day:

7:30 a.m.	Potty break.
7:40 a.m.	Feed puppy breakfast.
7:50 a.m.	Potty break. Put puppy in crate.
8:30 a.m.	Owner leaves for work.
12:30 p.m.	Neighbor gives puppy potty break.
12:40 p.m.	Neighbor gives puppy mid-day meal.
12:45 p.m.	Neighbor gives puppy potty break. Puts puppy in crate.
5:30 p.m.	Owner arrives home. Potty break.
6:30 p.m.	Potty break.
7:30 p.m.	Feed puppy dinner.
7:40 p.m.	Potty break.
9:00 p.m.	Potty break. Take up water so that puppy can better hold bladder all night.
10:00 p.m.	Final potty break. Puppy goes in crate for the night.

When housetraining, attach a leash to your puppy and take her outside to go.

traveling, on bad weather days when she can't play outside, or on those days when you're just in a hurry.

How To Deal With Setbacks

Your goal is to get your puppy to eliminate outside each and every time. But there are bound to be times when your puppy has accidents in the house. It's important to deal with these correctly so that you don't create further training problems.

Old-fashioned training used to recommend rubbing a puppy's nose in the mess or even spanking her. However, these methods do not teach a puppy to eliminate outside. Instead, they can teach her to be afraid of her owner. These old-fashioned techniques also can cause aggression in puppies because they simply don't understand why their owners are so upset. Peeing and pooping are natural puppy body functions. When you overreact to something your puppy has to do, she may react aggressively to defend herself.

If you find an accident in the house, and you did *not* catch your puppy eliminating, then there's nothing you can do but clean it up. Think about what went wrong. Did you or your family not supervise your puppy adequately? Does she need more frequent potty breaks? Did you veer from the routine feeding or daily schedule? Just find the mistake and fix it, then continue with your training.

If you do catch your dog having an accident, use your voice to interrupt the behavior with a sharp "No!" That's all you need. Immediately leash your puppy and take her outside, following your regular housetraining program. Be sure to praise her if she finishes pottying outside. Your goal is to make things very clear; you're upset when she eliminates inside, but you're thrilled when she eliminates outside. When you bring her back inside, don't yell at her again. Remember, timing is important when training your puppy. If you yell at her when she comes back inside, she could think that you're upset with her for coming into the house. Even though you're still upset that she had an accident in the house, her puppy attention span has long since moved on to other things.

When you clean up any accidents in the house, be sure to use a pet enzymatic cleaner. If you use vinegar or regular carpet cleaners, *you* won't be able to smell your puppy's mess, but *she* still can. Using a proper cleaner will help to prevent her from coming back to the same spot again and again.

It's typical for a puppy to have accidents during housetraining. She'll do fine for a couple weeks, and you'll think you're set, and then you'll find a puddle somewhere. Your puppy is young, and you're both learning the program, so be patient. If you stick to the program, you'll have a housetrained adult dog for life.

COLLAR AND LEASH TRAINING

If you ever want your puppy to go anywhere with you, she'll have to get used to a collar and leash. She is likely to follow you around closely until about four months of age. That's when she'll start developing better senses of smell and hearing and start noticing that the world is a bigger place than the view from behind your ankles. One day, your puppy will bolt for the street, something she's never done before. Don't wait for disaster to happen—collar and leash train your puppy right from the start.

Collar and Leash Training: The Basics

STEP 1:

a) First, train your puppy to become used to a collar. Get some treats ready. Put the collar on your puppy.

b) As soon as the collar is secure, give your puppy a treat and praise her.

c) It's normal for your puppy to scratch at her collar or act concerned about this new thing around her neck. Just ignore this. As long as you can get two fingers underneath it, it's not too tight. Redirect her behavior by getting her to play with a toy. Don't pet or soothe her if she's upset about the collar, or you will be rewarding that behavior, and she'll keep doing it. Also, don't take the collar off if she's scratching at it. This will just teach her that scratching gets the collar off. Be patient—your puppy will get used to it.

STEP 2:

a) Connect her leash to the collar, but don't hold onto it. Give her a treat. Just let her drag the leash around for a few minutes.

Supervise her very closely during this process so that she doesn't get tangled in anything.

b) Play with her. Don't let her chew on her leash. Just redirect her behavior by getting her to play with a toy.

STEP 3:

a) When your puppy is calm and not scratching at her collar or leash, take them off. Wait at least 15 minutes, then repeat Steps 1 to 3. Always give her a treat when you put her collar and leash on. Gradually increase the amount of time your puppy wears them. Always supervise your puppy when she's dragging the leash.

STEP 4:

a) Put your puppy's collar and leash on, then give her a treat. This time, gently hold the leash. Your puppy may not like it at first—she's used to being able to go wherever she wants. Don't soothe or pet her if she pulls against the leash, or you'll be rewarding that behavior. Ignore her instead. The second she stops, praise her. Redirect her behavior by getting her to play with a toy.

b) Take a short walk with your puppy, encouraging her to come with you. If she puts on the brakes, ignore this. She'll keep doing it if you make a fuss over her. Just pick up a toy or act very interested in something ahead of you. When your puppy realizes that she's not getting any attention, she'll want to join you. As soon as she does, give her a treat and praise her.

As soon as your puppy realizes that her leash means she's going outside or for a walk, she'll come to love it.

Leash Training: Next Steps

Some puppies love their leashes so much that they use them for leverage. They'll drag you down the block before you can brace yourself! Pulling on the leash is a very common problem. You will make this behavior worse if you reward it—and you may be rewarding it without even realizing it.

Let's say you drop some treats on the floor, and your puppy pulls you over to the treats, then gobbles them up. Your puppy just got paid for pulling on leash. What if you are walking your puppy, and you see a friend up ahead? Your puppy pulls you to your friend, who showers her with attention. Your puppy just got rewarded for pulling on the leash.

Before you can change your puppy's behavior, you have to change your own. Make sure that you aren't accidentally rewarding your puppy for pulling on leash, or the habit will be harder to fix.

STEP 1:

a) In your mind, imagine exactly where you want your puppy to walk next to you. Do you want her on your right side or your left? If you don't teach her a specific side, she could zigzag in front of you and cause you to trip. Do you want her right next to your leg? Or maybe a little ahead of you? Think of the exact place you want your puppy as a picture frame. When she steps outside the frame, she's out of the picture you want. Be sure that your entire family has the same picture in mind, or your puppy will get confused.

b) Pick a cue to use for this specific action, like "Let's go" or "Let's walk."

c) Start by practicing this exercise in a quiet area. It will be too much to ask your puppy to walk nicely by your side in a busy park. Start in a quiet environment, like your living room or backyard.

STEP 2:

a) Hold six small treats in your hand. Attach your puppy's leash. Use a treat to lure her to the side on which you want her to walk next to you. (Don't use the leash to drag her into position.) You can use your "Sit" cue if she knows it, or use this as a training opportunity to work on that exercise, too.

b) Give your cue "Let's go." Take one small step, and give your puppy a treat. Be sure to hold your hand low, in front of her nose, by your side. This can seem awkward at first, but if you hold your hand in front of your body, she'll cut in front of you. If you hold the treat too high, she'll start jumping. Hold the treat where you want your puppy's head to be.

c) Practice this for one week, several times a day. You are teaching your

Collar and leash training will teach your puppy to walk nicely next to you.

puppy that she'll get rewarded for staying next to you.

STEP 3:

a) Now it's time to start weaning your puppy off the treats. Attach her leash and get her positioned on the appropriate side. Ask her to sit. Give your cue "Let's go."

b) Instead of giving one treat for one step, take several steps before you give her a treat. Try not to hover your hand in front of her nose anymore. Instead, keep it up next to your waist. This will help to transition her attention from your hand to your side; you want her to learn to walk next to you, not to follow your hand around.

c) Watch your puppy—where is she walking in your imaginary picture frame?

- If your puppy walks *perfectly* where you pictured her to be, mark with a "Yes" and treat every couple steps. (Learn about the marker cue on page 87.)

- If your puppy lags *behind*, encourage her to keep up with you. Every time she comes up to your side, mark with a "Yes" and give her a treat.

- If your puppy *pulls*, immediately stop walking. Start again at Step 3, except this time, don't walk as far. The goal is to have a nice walk for three steps, then four steps, then more, gradually building toward success.

If your puppy puts on the brakes and refuses to walk with you, ignore her; as soon as she realizes that you're not paying attention to her, she'll want to join you.

STEP 4:

a) As your puppy learns to walk nicely by your side, gradually begin to increase the distractions in your environment. Go for walks around the block or in the park. You may have to back up your training a bit at first, but your puppy will catch on if you are consistent. If you find that your puppy is just too distracted, go back to a quieter place and gradually increase the distractions at a slower rate.

BASIC CUES

Teaching your puppy some basic cues will help to make your lives easier. These basics are the foundation for family manners. Keep these concepts in mind before you start:

- Puppies do not understand what you are saying unless you teach them what the words mean.
- Saying a cue over and over again isn't going to teach your puppy what the word means. Instead, you need to say the cue, then show your puppy what you want.
- Saying a cue really loud or in a mean voice isn't going to help ingrain it in your puppy's brain faster. She can hear you; she's just easily distracted. This is completely normal. Always use a friendly tone of voice when you give your puppy a cue. That way, you can reserve your stern voice for when she's done something wrong. If you use your stern voice all the time, you won't have anything to fall back on when you need to indicate your displeasure.
- Puppies learn best in short doses. Three 5-minute sessions are better than one 15-minute session, especially if your puppy is very young. If she starts losing interest in you, you've pushed her too hard. Always end a training session with her wanting more.
- Start training your puppy in family manners as soon as you bring her home. If you feel that you're already behind, don't worry. It's never too late to train your dog.

The Marker

The first thing to teach your puppy is a marker. This is a sound that marks the very instant in time when she did what you wanted her to do. In other words, it's a signal for when she got something right.

Why can't you just say "Good girl?" You can, but those words take longer to say than a quick marker cue. For example, let's say you ask your puppy to sit. She does. In the time it takes you to say that "Good girl," she could have already leaped up and spun around twice! So she might think that you are rewarding her for getting up or for spinning, but you want to reward her for sitting. Teaching your puppy a marker will significantly help her learn faster because it's more specific.

Your marker can be the sound from a clicker. The advantages

Training Treats

For training purposes, treats should be small and easy to swallow. Your puppy doesn't need an entire hot dog for sitting on cue—just a small sliver of a hot dog will do just fine. Your goal is not to fill your puppy up on treats, just to reward her for good behaviors.

Make sure that she really enjoys the treats that you choose. As your exercises or the distractions get harder, use more tantalizing treats. For example, if you're working in the quiet of your living room, her regular kibble may work great. In the middle of a busy park, kibble may not be enough to cut through the clutter of distractions, so you may have to use a more tempting treat.

to using a clicker are that it offers a unique sound, and it's precise. You also can use a short word, such as "yes." The advantages to using a verbal marker are that it's always handy, and you don't have to carry another piece of equipment, which can be challenging if you're also holding your puppy's leash and treats.

Be sure to only use the marker as a marker—don't try to make it several things, or your puppy will become confused. If you use the clicker to mark the desired behavior, for example, don't use it to also get your dog to come to you. If you do, it will no longer be a marker cue, and you will lose the power of that sound to indicate to your puppy that she has done something correctly.

STEP 1:

Have five treats in your hand. Make sure that you're close enough to your puppy to be able to give her treats easily.

STEP 2:

Don't ask her to sit or to come to you or anything else. You don't want her to associate any other actions with the marker. Just let her be there in front of you. Click your clicker one time, or say "Yes" one time and immediately give your puppy a treat. Only use the marker once, then follow it with a treat.

STEP 3:

Repeat four more times. Do this a couple times a day. Soon, you will find that your puppy gets excited at the marker sound.

Tip: Although you don't want to confuse your puppy and ask her to sit or down or anything else when you teach her the marker, you don't want to reward her for bad behavior, either. So, if she's jumping on you or pawing at you, wait until she stops. Then, give your marker and a treat. If you mark when she's jumping, her jumping may become worse.

The Release Cue

When you teach your puppy other cues, you're also going to use a universal release cue. This will indicate to her that the exercise is over, and she can stop doing whatever it is you asked her to do.

Teaching a release cue helps to prevent some common mistakes in training. For example, if you teach your puppy to sit, how does she know when she can get up again? The release cue tells her when to end the *sit*. Otherwise, you may end up with a puppy who sits for a few seconds, gets up, sits when you resay the cue, and gets up—over and over again.

Teach your puppy to pay attention with the watch me *cue and some treats.*

Use the same release cue for every exercise. When the exercise is finished, simply say "Okay" as your release cue. (You can choose a different, short word if you want. Just use the same release cue every time.) Make sure that you only use this cue to indicate that the exercise is over.

When you use your release word, make it very casual; do not praise your puppy or give her a treat afterward. Remember, you want to mark the second she performs the behavior and reward her *during* the behavior, not afterward. For example, let's say that you ask your puppy to lie down, and you correctly mark and praise the behavior. Then you release her with "Okay!" and give her pets and hugs. The next time you ask her to lie down, she may pop right back up because she enjoyed the affection she got the last time she got up. To avoid this, make sure that she gets all your attention *while* she's lying down, which is the behavior you wanted. When you release her with "Okay," be very matter-of-fact about it and don't show her much attention. She'll want you to ask her to do something else!

By simply learning when to shower your dog with attention and when to withhold it, you can encourage good behaviors.

Pay Attention

Have you ever been to a very busy city? Do you remember what it was like to have your senses bombarded for the first time with all the sights, smells, and sounds? Think of your puppy as living there, in that initial overwhelming moment, just about all the time.

Puppies have more acute senses than do people. Because they can smell and hear things that you can't, their environments are very rich. This also explains why they are so easily distracted. It's very normal for a puppy to pay close attention to you one second, then completely forget that you exist the next. Something as simple as a clod of dirt could completely enchant your puppy and capture her attention.

This is why it's a good idea to teach your puppy a cue for paying attention.

STEP 1:

Have some treats in your hand. Show your puppy a treat, and give her the cue "Watch me." Draw the treat up to your eyes. When she looks you in the eye (she'll really be looking at the treat, but that's okay) mark "Yes!" and give her the treat.

STEP 2:

After a couple repetitions, your puppy should be following the treat up to your eyes and looking at your face. At this point, stop holding a treat up to your eyes but continue to use your same hand signal. Draw your empty hand up to your eyes. When she looks you in the eye, mark "Yes!" and give her a treat.

Sitting for Attention

It's a good idea to only let people pet your puppy when she's sitting, especially if she's going to grow up to be a medium- or large-sized dog. If you start this habit now, she'll grow up to be a dog who goes up to people and sits for attention, which makes a great impression!

Use the training steps in this chapter to get your puppy to sit. Then, let people pet your puppy. If she gets up, they should immediately stop giving her any attention until she sits again. If you do this consistently, she'll learn that the only way she gets the attention she craves is to keep her rear on the ground.

It can be harder to train your friends and family than your puppy. Some may laugh or encourage your puppy to jump on them, which will just confuse her and undo all your training. Try to stick to the routine so that your puppy learns to greet her human friends with nice manners.

STEP 3:

When your puppy is looking you in the eyes regularly when you give her the cue, you can gradually wean off the hand signal if you choose.

Sit

Teaching your puppy to sit will solve a lot of behavioral issues. A puppy can't bolt out the door if she's sitting. She can't jump on your guests if she's sitting, either.

STEP 1:

a) Hold a treat in one hand by your puppy's nose. Give the cue "Fluffy, sit." Use a friendly voice. Slowly move the treat between her eyes, up over her head, back toward her shoulders. You're luring her into the right position, and you're also teaching her a hand signal. Only go as fast as her nose follows. If your treat is over her back, and she's looking straight ahead, you've lost her. Try again.

Use a treat to lure your puppy into a sit.

b) As your puppy's head goes up to follow the treat, her rear should lower to the ground. Keep watch. The second she sits, mark "Yes!" and give her the treat.

STEP 2:

a) Praise her for a few seconds, but be sure to use a soft voice. If your voice is too enthusiastic, she may be tempted to get up in excitement.

b) Release her with your "Okay!" cue. Do not reward her at this time—all her rewards should come when she's sitting, not when she's getting up.

When your puppy is sitting for a few seconds, it's time to train her to sit for longer periods. It's also time to stop using a treat as a lure to get her to sit. You will still give her a treat to reward her for sitting.

STEP 3:

a) Have some treats ready in one hand. Give the cue to sit. With an empty hand, use the same motion you've been using all along: Start at your puppy's nose, and go between her eyes and up over her head toward her shoulders.

Puppies learn hand signals before they learn verbal ones. While your puppy may not have quite figured out that the word "sit" means that you want her to place her rear on the ground, she may understand that your hand motion over her head means that very thing.

b) When she sits, mark "Yes!" Take a treat from your other hand and give it to her.

c) Watch your puppy closely. She'll tell you if she's going to get up. Is her ear twitching? Is she looking or leaning away from you? Is she starting to sniff the ground? These are all signs that she's growing bored or getting distracted. If you see them, take action quickly. *Before* she moves, mark "Yes!" and give her another treat. This will teach her that she gets rewarded the longer she sits.

d) Repeat Step C a few times, then release with "Okay!"

e) Gradually work up to longer times. Don't rush it. Smaller steps in training mean bigger results.

Troubleshooting: What if your puppy gets up before you've given the release cue? Don't tell her to sit again, and don't tell her "No!" or make an "Acck!" reprimand. She'll just interpret this as attention, and you only want to give her attention for performing the behavior, not getting up. Instead, lure her back into position. Slowly move the treat between her eyes, up over her head, and back toward her shoulders. The second she sits, mark "Yes!" and give her the treat. Next time, don't wait so long between rewards. You may have pushed her too far, too fast. Back up a bit and gradually work up to longer times.

What's a Clicker?

Clickers come in a variety of shapes, but the most common kind looks like a small, rectangular box. When you press a clicker, it makes a sharp "click" sound. You can teach your dog that this sound means that she has done something correctly. Clickers are available at pet retailers.

Sit: Next Steps

Once your puppy learns to sit, make it a part of her everyday life.

- Ask her to sit while you prepare her food. Set the food bowl down, then release her with "Okay!" so that she can eat.
- Ask her to sit at the door. Open the door, then release her with "Okay!"
- Ask her to sit in her crate while you open the crate door. Once you open the crate door, release her to come out of her crate with "Okay!"

If you train your puppy using everyday life situations, she'll learn manners for those situations. You'll end up with a puppy who sits at doors, sits for her food, and sits to be petted.

Troubleshooting: What if your puppy gets up before you've set the food bowl down or opened the door? If she gets up before you've

When teaching the down, *put a treat in front of your puppy's nose and slowly move it toward the floor. If she lays down, reward her with the treat.*

put the bowl down, just hold it back up and say nothing. If she gets up before you've released her to go out the door, just quickly shut the door again. (Don't catch her in it!) Give her a few seconds to figure it out. If she doesn't, use your hand signal to remind her to sit. Then, start to lower the bowl or open the door again. If she gets up again, hold the bowl back up or shut the door again. She'll soon learn that nothing happens unless she's sitting.

Down

Lying down is a great behavior to teach your puppy. If she's going to grow up to be a large dog, she won't be as intimidating to some people if she's lying down. It's also a convenient position in which to trim your puppy's nails.

STEP 1:

a) Have a treat in your hand. Give the cue "Fluffy, sit." Don't forget to use your hand signal. Mark "Yes!" when she sits.

b) Put the treat in front of your puppy's nose. Give the cue "Fluffy, down." (Use a friendly voice!) Move the treat down her chest. Go very, very slowly. Only go as fast as her nose follows. If you're holding the treat on the floor, and she's looking up at your face, you've lost her. Try again.

c) When her head follows the treat down to the floor, slowly move the treat along the floor outward and away from her. She should lie down to get the treat. You're also teaching her a hand signal at the same time.

d) When she lies down, mark "Yes!" and give her the treat.

STEP 2:

a) Praise her for a few seconds in a soft voice. If you're too enthusiastic, she may be encouraged to get up. It also may not be a good idea to pet your puppy during this exercise. Some puppies get too excited when you pet them, and they pop right up. If your puppy is one of them, save the petting for later and just use a friendly voice to reward her for lying down nicely.

b) Release her with "Okay!"

Troubleshooting: What if your puppy follows the treat, but her rear pops up? Instead of moving the treat along the floor, away from her, try moving it inward, in between her front paws. Go really, really slowly. Some puppies prefer to "fold" into a down position. If you're still having trouble, exercise your puppy so that she's good and tired, then try the exercise again. She may be more likely to lie down if she's not bouncing with energy.

Down: Next Steps

When your puppy is lying down for a few seconds, it's time to train her to lie down for longer periods. It's also time to stop using a treat as a lure to get her to lie down. You will still give her a treat to reward her for performing the cue.

STEP 1:

a) Have some treats ready in one hand. Give the cue "Fluffy, sit." Use your hand signal. Mark "Yes!" when she sits.

b) Give the cue "Fluffy, down." With an empty hand, start at her nose, go down her chest, and move your hand along the floor, away from her (or toward her if that's her preference) until she lies down. When she lies down, mark "Yes!" Take a treat from your other hand and give it to her. While she's chewing, stand up quickly. Your goal is to have her lying down while you stand up.

c) Watch your puppy closely. She'll tell you if she's going to get up. Is she fidgety? Is she looking away from you? Is she starting to sniff the ground? These are all signs that she's growing bored or getting distracted. If you see them, take action quickly. *Before* she moves, mark "Yes!" and give her another treat. This will teach her that she gets rewarded the longer she lies down.

d) Repeat Step C a few times, then release with "Okay!"

e) Gradually work up to longer times.

Troubleshooting: What if your puppy gets up before you give the release cue? Don't tell her "Down" again, and don't tell her "No!" or make an "Acck!" reprimand. Instead, lure her back into position. Start at her nose and slowly move your hand down along her chest, then along the floor, away from her. The second she lies down, mark "Yes!" and give her the treat. Next time, don't wait so long between rewards. She may need more feedback to understand what you want.

Teaching your puppy some basic obedience cues will help to cement the bond between the two of you.

Come

Getting your puppy to come when you call her is one of the most important things you can teach her. Not only will it save you the trouble of chasing her, but it could save her life!

Coming to you must always be pleasant for your puppy. And her idea of what's pleasant is the one that counts. Let's say she's been rolling around in the dirt and smells awful, and you want to give her a bath, but she hates baths. If you say "Fluffy, come!" and she races to you, only to be plopped in the bathtub, she'll remember it was an unpleasant experience. The next time you say "Fluffy, come!" she'll probably think, "Eek! Bath time!" and run away. Instead of teaching her to come when you call her, you just taught her to run *away* from you. If you ever have to do something to your puppy that she will find unpleasant, get some treats and go to your puppy, instead of calling her to come to you.

Many puppy owners also make the mistake of calling their puppies to punish them. "Come over here so I can yell at you!" Why would they do that? This only teaches a dog that coming to you is a bad idea. You want to teach your puppy the opposite—that coming to you is always a good thing. It's like your boss sending you a message like "Come to this meeting, and I'll dock your pay!" versus "Come to this meeting and get a raise!" Which meeting would you rather attend?

STEP 1:

a) Put your puppy on leash and have some treats in your hand. Walk in one direction, and let her get a bit distracted.

b) Give the cue "Fluffy, come!" (Use a friendly voice!) Immediately start running backward. (You'll still be facing your original direction; you'll just be going in reverse.) If you are not comfortable running, that's fine. Still reverse direction, and go as fast as you are comfortably able. Puppies usually love to chase things, so when you start moving backward, your puppy should run toward you. Don't jerk the leash on her neck. Instead, encourage her to run to you.

STEP 2:

a) After about 10 feet (3.0 m), stop moving. When your puppy reaches you, mark "Yes!" and give her treat. Pet and praise her.

b) Release with "Okay!"

Troubleshooting: Does your puppy already think that the cue "Come!" means "Chase me around the yard"? If so, start with a clean slate. Pick a different cue, such as "Here!"

Keep your puppy on leash so that you can minimize distractions. If you're in a fenced-in yard but not attached to your puppy, and you call her to come to you but halfway there she gets distracted by a butterfly, you're just setting yourself up to fail. Set yourself up to succeed by staying attached. It takes a lot of training to teach a dog to come off leash, especially with distractions around. Remember, puppies learn best in gradual steps.

Come When Called: Next Steps

When your puppy is regularly running to you when you give her the cue, it's time for you to rest easy and stop running backward. You also can polish the behavior by training your puppy to sit when she gets to you.

STEP 1:

a) Walk with your puppy. Give the cue "Fluffy, come!" and walk backward.

b) Encourage her to run to you. Your goal is to slow down while your puppy still comes to you quickly.

STEP 2:

a) After about 10 feet (3.0 m), stop moving. When your puppy

reaches you, give her the cue "Fluffy, sit!" Use the previous lessons if she's still learning this behavior.

b) When she sits, mark "Yes!" and give her a treat.

c) Release with "Okay!"

d) Repeat Steps 1 and 2 until your puppy is coming reliably.

STEP 3:

a) Gradually add distance between you and your puppy so that she has farther to come to you. You can get a really long leash for this, or practice in a closed room where few distractions are present.

Having your puppy come when called could one day save her life.

Puppies learn in gradual steps, so take your time. When your dog does well, start practicing outdoors, in the neighborhood (always on leash for safety), and gradually add more distractions. If you find that she's easily distracted or is getting confused, you may have to break down your training into smaller steps.

Leave It

Puppies explore the world with their mouths. There may be days when you feel as if you brought a vacuum cleaner home rather than a puppy! They may pick up some items that are safe, some that may annoy you—and some that could hurt them. Your puppy won't know the difference, so it's important to teach her cues to keep her safe.

One of the best cues that you can teach your puppy is "Leave it." This is a *preventive* cue. It's always best to prevent your puppy from getting hold of something rather than waiting until she already has it in her mouth. Every time she gets hold of something she's not supposed to, she's practicing that behavior. And that's not something you want her to improve. Also, some items may be so dangerous that you don't want your puppy near them at all in the first place. For example, if you spill something hot off the stove onto the floor, "Drop it" isn't going to help your puppy. You

want her to leave the spill alone altogether so that she doesn't get burned. You may find that, with a growing puppy, "Leave it" is your favorite cue!

STEP 1:

a) Have treats in both hands. Your right hand will be your Temptation Hand—you'll be showing your puppy the treat you have in this hand. Your left hand will serve as your Delivery Hand—you'll give her treats with this hand.

b) Hold your Delivery Hand behind your back.

c) Hold your Temptation Hand right under your puppy's nose and show her the treat in your palm. Let her see it, but don't let her take it. Immediately close your hand into a fist so that she can't get the treat. Give the cue "Leave it." Don't use a mean voice! This is information, not discipline. Use a friendly voice to train your puppy.

d) Your puppy will sniff, lick, paw, and maybe even chew on your hand. Don't say anything. Don't repeat "Leave it! Leave it! Leave it!" over and over. Just wait it out. Be patient.

STEP 2:

a) Your puppy will eventually realize that she cannot get the treat out of your hand. She may sniff the ground to see if you dropped the treat. She may get distracted by a noise elsewhere, or she may just sit and look at you, puzzled. Just be patient—she will give up. The *second* she moves away from your Temptation Hand, for any reason, mark "Yes!" You are marking the very instant she leaves your hand alone.

b) Immediately bring your Delivery Hand around and give your puppy a treat from that hand.

STEP 3:

a) Repeat this exercise several times in a row several times a day.

b) Practice in every room of your home, especially your bathroom and kitchen, which are likely places you will drop things that you don't want your puppy to get. Practice in your front yard and back yard as well, and have your puppy on leash so that you can control her distractions.

c) When your puppy is quickly leaving your hand alone when you say "Leave it" and looking for the other hand to deliver a treat, it's time to switch hands. Make your left hand the Temptation Hand and your right hand the Delivery Hand. Know that your puppy will initially be confused and may go back to licking or pawing at your new Temptation Hand. This is normal, because you've changed the rules of the game on her. Just be patient. She'll learn!

Leave It: Next Steps

When your puppy is easily leaving both hands alone in a variety of locations, it's time to make the challenge a bit harder. Don't rush into this step. If your puppy still needs some practice, take your time and help her learn what you want. Otherwise, she may get confused, and you'll undo all your hard work so far.

Puppies often find objects that fall on the floor more tempting than ones just sitting there. They are attracted to movement. Until now, you've held a treat to tempt your puppy. Now you're going to start teaching her to leave a dropped item alone.

STEP 1:

a) Have treats in both hands. Show your puppy one of the treats and drop it on the floor. Immediately cover it with your foot and give the cue "Leave it." Don't let her get it, and don't step on your puppy!

b) Your puppy will sniff, lick, paw, and maybe even try to chew your foot. Don't say anything. Don't repeat "Leave it! Leave it! Leave it!" over and over. Just wait it out. Be patient.

A Two-Handed Approach

Puppy owners make two common mistakes when teaching the *leave it* exercise.

1. **Pulling the Temptation Hand away when giving the cue.** If you say "Leave it" and pull your hand away from your puppy, that's not going to teach her to leave something alone. It will teach her that you won't let her grab something in the first place. This is like doing her homework for her. You want her to learn to leave items alone on her own, without you grabbing them away from her. If you were to drop something tempting on the floor, like a juicy steak, you may not be able to pull it away. Be sure that you keep your hand still. Just close your hand into a fist so that your puppy can't get the treat.

2. **Distracting your puppy with your Delivery Hand.** Some people are so eager to give their puppy the marker cue that they move their Delivery Hand around too soon, crinkle a treat bag, or make some motion that ends up distracting their puppy. If you distract your puppy from temptation, that's also doing her homework for her. If you were to drop a steak on the floor, you may not have a pork chop in your hand to tease your puppy away from it! Don't distract your puppy away from your Temptation Hand. Let her learn to leave it alone on her own. Be ready to mark and reward her the second that she does.

The drop it *cue teaches your puppy to relinquish an item that she already has in her mouth.*

c) The *second* she moves away from your foot for any reason, mark "Yes!" You are marking the very instant she leaves your foot alone.

STEP 2:

a) Repeat this exercise several times in a row, several times a day.

b) Practice in every room of your home, especially your bathroom and kitchen, which are likely places where you will drop things that you don't want your puppy to get. Practice in your front yard and back yard as well, and have your puppy on leash so that you can control her distractions.

Troubleshooting: What if, after you've practiced this exercise a few times, your puppy doesn't even try to get the temptation treat anymore? This means that she is a quick learner! Be sure to mark "Yes!" and reward her for leaving the treat alone altogether.

What if your puppy is about to grab something, you say "Leave it," and she grabs it anyway? A rolled-up sock or your child's stuffed bear may be more valuable to your puppy than the treats you've been practicing with for this exercise. Keep practicing your "Leave it" cue, and gradually work up to some really tempting items. Always remember to reward your puppy with an item of greater value than the item she leaves alone. For example, if your puppy leaves a rolled-up sock alone and you pay her with a piece of plain kibble, she may think it wasn't worth it. But if you pay her with a piece of liver, she'll remember that next time and will be more likely to leave the item alone again.

Drop It and Take It

Even though you'll teach your puppy to "leave it," there are bound to be times when she's so fast, she'll grab something before you have a chance to get the right words out of your mouth. What if your puppy gets into the hamper and grabs a sock? What if she nabs your child's toy and runs under the bed? Once she has an item in her mouth, it's too late for "Leave it." She already has it. This is where "Drop it" comes in; you want to teach her to spit items out if necessary. To teach a good "Drop it" cue, team it with "Take it."

STEP 1:

a) Get an item that your puppy will likely take in her mouth, like a favorite toy. Have some really good treats handy.

b) Give the cue "Fluffy, take it!" (Use a friendly voice!) Offer the item to your puppy. When she takes it, mark "Yes!" You don't have to give her a treat at this time because getting the item itself is a reward.

STEP 2:

a) Show your puppy the treat. Give the cue "Drop it!" Don't use a threatening voice for this. You're not trying to scare her, just teach her.

b) Hold an open hand under your puppy's mouth to catch the item. If your treat was tempting enough, she should drop the item to eat the treat. When she drops the item, mark "Yes!" and give her the treat. Praise her.

c) You can gradually move your hand away so that your puppy has to move to put the item in your hand. If she drops the item, and it doesn't land in your hand, just say "Take it" again. Hold your hand out toward her. Don't mark "Yes" until the item lands in your hand. If she tries twice without success, you're proceeding too fast for your puppy. Back up your training and use more gradual steps.

Practice this exercise every day. It could save your puppy's life!

Troubleshooting: What if your puppy won't give up the item? You need a different combination—an item she finds of lesser value and a treat she finds of higher value. It may take you a few tries to find the right match, but you can do it.

What if your puppy growls when you try this exercise? If she growls over her toys, bones, or other items, please seek the assistance of a professional reward-based trainer. This problem is

Choose one toy to use in tug-of-war; you don't want your puppy to learn to tug all her toys or other objects.

called *resource guarding*, and it must be addressed early before it gets worse. Your puppy must learn that you control all the items in her world. You can teach her that without using harsh methods, which could make the problem more serious. Get professional help.

The Ultimate Take It and Drop It: Tug-of-War

Before teaching your puppy how to play tug-of-war, review these rules:

1. Your puppy should already know and respond to your "Take it" and "Drop it" cues. Don't start playing tug-of-war until your puppy quickly takes and drops items when you give the cues. If she enjoys playing "keep-away," you need to practice those exercises first.

2. Only one toy must be designated for tug-of-war. You don't want your puppy to learn to tug all her toys or other objects. By sticking to one toy only, it will be easier for her to understand that this is the only toy that she can play the game with.

3. Your puppy cannot play tug unless you give the "Tug" cue. If she grabs the tug toy in your hand before invited, the game's over.

4. All cues to "Drop it" during the game must be followed. If your puppy does not drop the tug toy on cue, the game's over.

5. Take frequent obedience breaks. Follow a "Drop it" with some

manners exercises, such as *sit*, *down*, or *stay* before starting the tug game again.

6. If your puppy makes contact with her teeth on your skin for any reason, even if by accident, the game's over.

By following the rules, you will be teaching your puppy how to play tug-of-war safely. This is a very important lesson to teach her now. If you have a puppy who will grow up to be a large dog, you especially don't want to wait until she has her adult teeth and strength to understand how to use them safely around people.

Now that you know the rules, here's how to teach tug-of-war:

STEP 1:

a) Offer your puppy the designated tug toy. Tell her "Take it."

b) When she takes the toy, give the cue "Tug" and start pulling on the toy. Encourage her to tug back. If she does, mark "Yes!" and praise her.

STEP 2:

a) Play tug for a while, then give her the "Drop it" cue. When she drops it, mark "Yes!" and praise her.

b) Repeat Steps 1 and 2. Occasionally, when she drops the toy, give her cues for some of her family manners, such as *sit* or *down*. When she performs the behavior, mark "Yes!" and then give her the cues to "Take it" and "Tug" again as her reward.

Troubleshooting: What if your puppy breaks one of the rules? If she grabs the toy and starts tugging before you gave her the proper cues, immediately say "Too bad!" and end the game. Ignore your puppy for a few minutes—do not lecture her, talk to her, or even make eye contact with her. Leave the room if you want, but don't do so if she can't be left unsupervised without getting into trouble or having a housetraining accident. After a few minutes, let her try again. If she again grabs at the toy and tugs before you invite her, immediately say "Too bad!" and end the game. Ignore her for another couple minutes, then try again later or the next day.

If she should make contact with her teeth on your skin, even by accident, immediately yelp "Ouch!" and end the game. Even if it didn't hurt, act like it did. This teaches your puppy to be very careful with her teeth. Completely ignore her for a few minutes. Don't lecture her about how she nipped you—the more you talk to your puppy, the more attention you're paying her. After ignoring her for a few minutes, let her try again. If she again makes contact with her teeth on your skin, immediately yelp "Ouch!" and end the game. Try again later or the next day.

If you are consistent about making your puppy follow the rules, she'll learn them.

OBEDIENCE CLASSES AND PUPPY KINDERGARTEN

Training Precision

Do you want your puppy to respond to cues immediately, the first time you give them? If you want this kind of performance, you have to train it. For example, if you say "Fluffy, sit! Sit! Sit! Sit down! Sitsitsitsit!" then that's what your puppy will learn. If you want your puppy to respond to just one "Sit!", only say the cue one time.

Your puppy won't learn to listen to you in other places if you only train her at home or in your yard. If she's never exposed to other people or dogs in a positive manner, she could be afraid when she encounters them later. This could cause her to act shy and nervous or to lash out to try to protect herself. A reward-based group class can be an excellent way to help you better understand your puppy, teach her manners, and get her used to other people and dogs.

Many people used to recommend that a puppy be at least six months old before starting classes. Modern knowledge of puppy learning and behavior now indicates that the earlier you start training your puppy, the better! It's true that she will have a short attention span and be easily distracted. But your young puppy is an eager sponge for learning. If you start training her now, you won't have as many bad habits to fix later.

Puppy kindergarten classes are especially geared for puppies of usually less than six months of age. A good puppy kindergarten class focuses on socialization, handling, and may even feature some playtime with other puppies. You'll learn how to deal with common puppy behaviors, such as mouthing, destructive chewing, and housetraining. Consider it a preschool for a basic family-manners class. Some instructors will require that your puppy has at least her first two sets of vaccinations before attending.

If you have a quality puppy kindergarten class available in your area, don't be afraid to get started. It's never too early to start training your dog. If you have a large-breed puppy, get her in class as soon as you are able. What might be a cute antic or slightly annoying issue now will only grow as your puppy grows.

If you don't have a good puppy kindergarten in your area, you may have to wait until she has had all her puppy shots before you can sign her up for a group class. This will be at about 15 to 16 weeks of age. Just as it's never too early to start training your puppy, it's never too late, either.

What to Look for in a Good Obedience Class

Not all obedience classes are alike. It's important to do your research and find a good class with a knowledgeable instructor. You don't want your impressionable puppy to have a bad experience. Here are some tips on how to find the right class for you and your family.

Interview the Instructor

Make sure that the instructor thoroughly understands the science of learning theory and canine behavior. Modern training techniques do not require the use of aversives, physical punishment, or harsh tools. The instructor should be very knowledgeable but able to teach you what he knows without using jargon or confusing terms. He should be a good educator of people, not just of dogs.

Ask for the trainer's credentials. If the instructor says that he is a "Master Dog Trainer" or "Certified Trainer," where did he earn the designation? Was it from one training school or from a professionally moderated national certification program? If the instructor says that he is a "behaviorist," ask exactly what training and education went into the title. The program for certified applied animal behaviorists (www.animalbehavior.org) is very stringent and requires specific educational and scientific credentials. A dog trainer who specializes in specific behavior issues is not the same as a certified applied animal behaviorist.

Some instructors have personal dogs with many impressive titles that they earned during obedience or agility competitions. This may be important to you if you wish to pursue competition with your puppy. Titles demonstrate that the instructor is good at training his own dogs, but how good is he at training other people to train their dogs? Ask about his students' success

A good obedience instructor will interact well with your puppy.

rates in the ring.

Ask if the trainer participates in regular continuing education. Does he take classes? Attend workshops and conferences in his field? Is he a member of any professional organizations, such as the Association of Pet Dog Trainers (APDT)? You don't want someone who's been training one way for 30 years because that's how he's always done it.

Because there are so many variables when training a puppy, an ethical dog trainer will not guarantee the results of his training. Puppies have different temperaments. Puppy owners have different levels of commitment and experience. It's impossible to guarantee results when so many factors contribute to training a puppy. For example, if an owner is too busy to do any of the class homework, then his puppy won't keep up with the class. An instructor doesn't go home with class members to guarantee that their puppies are being properly trained. What an instructor *can* do is guarantee satisfaction with his services. Be wary of those who guarantee that your puppy will learn specific behaviors or attain a certain level of training.

Get References

If you have friends with well-behaved dogs, ask them where they got their training. Ask your veterinarian, pet sitter, or groomer for referrals.

Observe a Class

A good instructor will welcome you to sit in and observe a class (without your puppy, of course). The class should be well organized. The instructor should be friendly but firm enough to keep the class under control and safe for people and puppies alike.

There should be a good ratio of instructors and assistants to students. That will vary depending on the area and types of dogs in the class, but in general, you should be able to see that each student is getting individualized attention.

Students and puppies should enjoy the classes. Training classes should be fun, not stern, boot camp drill exercises. Sure, occasionally owners will get frustrated, but a good instructor will motivate students to encourage their puppies, rather than get angry with them.

Instructors should do a good job of explaining and

demonstrating the exercises. Does he leave time for questions? Look for a trainer who treats his clients with respect and courtesy.

A good instructor will send home quality written materials so that students will have a better understanding of the exercises and be able to work on them at home. Do the students receive written handouts or homework? Are they clear and easy to understand?

Take your time to find the right class. Think about the teachers who made a difference in your life. You want a trainer who will make a difference in the life of you and your puppy, together.

Training a puppy can be great fun as you watch the lightbulb in her puppy brain go off and she begins to understand what you want. Don't let the fun end with puppyhood, though. If you don't keep up with training, you may find your puppy relaxing her behaviors or starting some undesirable ones. Just start your training sessions again so that both of you stay in practice. You may find that you want to continue teaching your puppy more and more!

Chapter

6

SOLVING

Puppy Problem Behaviors

Just as the way that you communicate is very different from how your puppy communicates, your perceptions can be different, too. What you think may be a problem may not feel like a problem at all to your puppy. In fact, she's probably having a great time!

Puppy mouthing, jumping up, barking, digging, and even eating poop are all quite enjoyable activities for your puppy. To us, they can be a nuisance (or in the case of poop eating, quite disgusting!). It's up to you to teach your puppy how you want her to behave. Fortunately, you can successfully resolve many behavior problems using reward-based methods.

WHAT IS A PUPPY PROBLEM BEHAVIOR?

A puppy problem behavior is a behavior that can be annoying or potentially harmful. It's a lot easier to address these problems now rather than later. The more chances that your puppy has to practice undesirable behaviors, the more ingrained they will become.

Some problem behaviors are obvious. If your puppy jumps on your guests, it's a problem. If she barks at every little sound she hears, it's a problem. But sometimes, puppy owners don't recognize problems until they become serious issues. Here are some tips for recognizing some commonly overlooked problem behaviors:

Anything That Won't Be Cute When Your Puppy Is Full Grown Isn't Cute Now

You may giggle when your Rottweiler puppy jumps up to kiss your chin, but will you still be giggling when your full-grown Rottie leaps up and clocks you in the jaw? If your Corgi puppy looks adorable pulling on your pant leg, will it be as cute years down the line and dozens of shredded pants later?

Any time your puppy does something, ask yourself

A well-behaved puppy is a joy to own.

"Will this be cute when she's an adult?" If the answer is no, it's a problem behavior. Start fixing the problem now. Your puppy will not understand if you laugh when she jumps up on you for the first few months, then suddenly get angry and yell at her when she's older and bigger. Don't change the rules later down the line —establish them now and avoid confusion and frustration later.

This can be challenging, because puppies really are adorable. But if you or your family members or friends giggle or laugh when your puppy does something, you're rewarding the behavior, so she will likely keep repeating it. Think of what you'll have to put up with in the future, and resist the temptation.

Aggressive Behavior of any Kind Is not Funny

It may be tempting to laugh if your tiny puppy growls over a toy when you try to take it, but this is actually a problem behavior. Growling over a food bowl, toys, or other "prizes" is called "resource guarding." This problem will not go away on its own, and actually is likely to become worse if not addressed. What starts out as a growl could end up as a snap or a bite.

Teasing your puppy while she growls is not a game. Instead, it's likely to increase her aggression. What if she gets hold of something dangerous, and you can't get it away from her because she snaps at you? What if a small child tries to take your puppy's "prize" away? Some puppies may not bite an adult but won't hesitate to bite a young child.

If your puppy is growling over items, it's no laughing matter. Call a professional dog trainer or applied animal behaviorist and get help addressing the problem now, before your puppy and her growls get any bigger.

There's another instance where puppy growling is a real concern. Some puppies growl at their tails, paws, or other parts of their own bodies. You may have even seen videos of this behavior on popular television shows or on the Internet. Many folks laugh out loud when they see a dog growling at herself, but experts in dog behavior cringe. This is not normal behavior for a dog, and it could indicate some serious problems. If your puppy is growling at herself, consult your veterinarian and a professional dog trainer or applied animal behaviorist.

Please note that this does not apply to a puppy who growls at her reflection in a mirror. It's very common for puppies to be startled at their reflections and growl as a result. If your puppy does this, touch the mirror and show her that there's not another dog there. Don't force her to go smell the mirror; she should approach it by herself. Most puppies figure this out quickly, and some even seem to admire what they see!

Obsessive Behavior Is Not Healthy

Some puppies chase their tails over and over again, so much so that you have to physically stop them or they'll spin until they drop. Some act like they're snapping at bugs, but you can't see any insects at all. Some puppies may chase reflections over and over. If your dog exhibits one of these behaviors, it's not a cute puppy antic. Please call your veterinarian for assistance. Your puppy may be ill and need professional help.

What Not to Do

So what if you decide that your puppy has a problem behavior? If you want to stop your puppy from doing something you don't like, do not:

- Knee her in the chest
- Scruff shake her
- Spank her
- Flip her upside down or "alpha roll" her
- Yell at her

If you use physical means to try to change your puppy's behavior, she may interpret your action as part of her game, so the behavior will actually get worse instead of better. (Have you ever seen two puppies or dogs playing together? They can play pretty roughly.) Or she won't engage in the problem behavior anymore because you frightened her. This will work great for you, but what about everyone else in your family? Can your five-year-old son

Bright Lights, Big Problem

You may find that your puppy loves to chase the beam of a flashlight or a laser light around the room. For some puppies, this is good exercise. But other puppies can develop obsessive behaviors over chasing lights. It can start with a laser, but then you notice that your puppy is chasing the reflection off your watch, or the mini blinds, or cars that pass by a window. Some puppies become so obsessed with chasing lights that they need medication to help them stop. Because there is a risk of your puppy developing a compulsion for chasing lights, it's best to avoid the light show altogether. Choose another game for your puppy.

effectively knee your puppy in the chest? Can your grandparents spank your puppy hard enough? You want your puppy to listen to everyone in the family, not just the person who is strongest.

Sometimes, using harsh methods to discipline a puppy can seriously backfire. If you frighten your dog enough, she may feel that she has to defend herself. This doesn't mean that she's stubborn or defying you—she's just frightened. For example, let's say your puppy jumps up on you and you spank her. She doesn't understand that you don't want her to jump up—she just understands that you are scary. So she growls at you to tell you that she's afraid and wants you to stop. You get really mad and spank her again. She figures that you didn't understand her message the first time, so she has to be clearer. She bites you. Is she a stubborn, willful puppy? No. You're both just communicating in very different ways. You're spanking her, because you want her to stop jumping. She's growling and biting, because she's afraid of your anger.

What to Do

You do not need to use harsh methods to discipline your puppy. Instead of getting angry with her for a problem behavior, teach her what you'd rather her do instead. For every behavior that your puppy does that you don't like, there are lots of preferable behaviors that you can teach her to engage in instead. For example, if you don't like your puppy jumping, teach her to sit when she greets people. Instead of getting mad at her for chasing the cat, teach her the *leave it* cue so that she leaves the cat alone. This is a much more effective way of communicating with your puppy and solving problem behaviors.

AGGRESSION

Aggression can be hard to define if you're not familiar with puppy behavior. For example, some owners worry that their puppies are aggressive because they mouth everything. All puppies mouth, and it's usually a normal behavior. Other owners worry when their puppies growl during playtime. Many puppies do this and don't have an aggressive bone in their bodies. So how do you know if your dog has an aggression problem? You may have an issue if your puppy growls or snaps:

- when you reach for her food bowl

- when you reach for her toy or chew bone or try to take them away from her
- when you try to brush her, pick her up, or move her off furniture
- when another dog approaches her or things that she perceives as hers

If your puppy does any of these things, she may have an aggression problem. Puppies can get aggression from their parents; if mom or dad was aggressive, their puppies could have inherited the trait. They also can be aggressive due to fear. Fearful puppies may lash out to protect themselves, figuring they'll get the scary monster before the monster gets them. Aggression can also be caused by using harsh disciplinary or training techniques. Or your puppy may have learned that growling gets her what she wants. There are a variety of reasons, and all of them are serious. Aggressive puppies can become aggressive dogs, and they can hurt people. If you have children in your life, an aggressive puppy can be of even greater concern. There is tremendous liability with aggression, so if you think that your puppy has this problem, don't delay.

If you suspect that your puppy is aggressive, take her to vet for a full checkup to make sure that the aggression isn't due to a physical problem.

What to Do

Take your puppy to the veterinarian for a full checkup to make sure that the aggression isn't due to a physical problem. If she is healthy, contact a professional reward-based trainer or applied animal behaviorist to assist you. He will personally evaluate your puppy and come up with a treatment plan.

What Not to Do

In the meantime, avoid these common mistakes:

- **Pretending there isn't a problem.** You love your puppy, and may be heartbroken or unwilling to admit that she has a problem. However, just because she is aggressive doesn't mean that she is evil. It's important to face the facts. Don't make excuses. ("I shouldn't have approached her when she had her bone" or "She was just tired.") Get help.

- **Punishing your puppy when she growls.** You may be tempted to yell at your puppy when she growls over her food bowl, for example, but that will not solve the problem. A growl is communication—your puppy is trying to tell you something. If you punish her when she growls, you're not eliminating the problem; you're eliminating the communication. The puppy may go straight to biting, rather than giving you the growl as a warning.
- **Exposing your puppy to her triggers.** It's very important that you carefully manage an aggressive puppy. If she's not good with children, do not take her to your child's soccer game in the hope that she'll get more used to children. You are risking a terrible incident. If your puppy growls over special toys, don't let her have them until you are trained in how to work with the problem. Manage her so that she doesn't have access to things that trigger an aggressive episode.

BARKING (EXCESSIVE)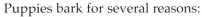

Some puppies like to talk more than others. You may not mind them barking for a bit when someone rings the doorbell or if someone comes into the yard, but too much barking can be a real problem. It's also a very common cause of neighbor complaints.

Some breeds are more prone to barking than others. Shetland Sheepdogs, Miniature Schnauzers, Samoyeds, terriers, and hounds tend to be more talkative. If you have one of these puppies, remember, she was your choice. You may not have known about this issue before you picked her out, but it's not her fault that her breed is chatty. This doesn't mean that you have to put up with excessive barking, though. You may need to stock up on extra patience for a breed with this tendency, because her genes will be telling her to talk while your training will be encouraging her to be quiet.

Puppies bark for several reasons:

- **They're bored.** They may have 100 toys available, but puppies can still be bored. It's like having satellite or cable television— there's hundreds of channels, but you still flip from channel to channel, trying to find something good to watch.

- **They're protective.** Some breeds are more likely to bark at people or animals approaching their "territory" than others.
- **They're afraid.** Some puppies can be startled by sounds or sights, and they're telling you that they're afraid by barking.
- **They're announcing something.** It could be a car going by, kids playing in the cul-de-sac, or a raindrop hitting a blade of grass. Some puppies feel a need to narrate things that they notice.
- **They're trying to tell you something.** All barking is communication. You may never figure out why your dog is barking, but she is definitely trying to say something to you.

What to Do

To stop excessive barking, choose a cue for quiet behavior. It can be "Quiet," "Hush," "Shhhhh," or whatever, as long as you and your family use the same cue every time for this specific action. Think of situations that are likely to get your puppy to bark. For example, does she bark when someone comes into the house? When you're preparing her dinner? To teach her to be quiet, she needs to engage in barking.

STEP 1:

a) Hide a treat in your hand.

b) Perform whatever action triggers your puppy's barking.

c) After about three barks, give your cue "Hush." Don't yell it. This is information, not discipline. She doesn't know what the word means yet, so yelling won't make it sink in faster.

d) Hold the treat near your puppy's nose so that she can smell it. She will stop barking to smell the treat. The second she stops barking, mark "Yes!" and give her the treat.

e) Repeat a couple times, then take a break and repeat the exercise later in the day.

STEP 2:

a) After your puppy has successfully stopped barking several times in a row, it's time to wean her off the treat in your hand. Repeat the exercise without holding the treat, but have it nearby. Just say "Hush" and wait. Don't repeat "Hush! Hush! Hush!" Just patiently wait for the barking to stop.

b) The second she stops barking, mark "Yes." Pick up the treat and give it to her. You can gradually work up to not having the

> ## Consistent Lessons Are Persistent Lessons
>
> Is everyone in your family on the same page in teaching your puppy good manners? If one member of your family thinks that it's fine for your puppy to mouth him, and even encourages it with roughhousing games, she will learn that that's how she should play with everyone. She won't understand that she can't do that with your toddler. Make sure that your entire family is following the same rules, or your puppy can't possibly learn what's expected.

treat nearby.

Troubleshooting: What if your puppy doesn't stop barking for the treat? Either the treat isn't good enough to outweigh the fun of barking, or your stimulus was too exciting. For example, the sound of the doorbell can send puppies into a tizzy. So, if you're using the doorbell sound as an introductory way to teach your puppy not to bark, then it may be too much at this point. Try another trigger, and work up to the doorbell.

What if your puppy stops to eat the treat, then goes right back to barking again? Show her another treat, say "Too bad!", and turn and walk away. She'll learn that she only gets one chance to earn a treat, and that she gets no attention for continuing barking.

Dealing With Different Triggers

Now that you're on your way to teaching a *quiet* cue, here's how to address some specific reasons why puppies tend to bark.

Barking Through Windows

Some puppies love to look out windows or doors and bark at everything they see. To stop this, use good management. Prevent your puppy from looking out the window and door. This may mean blocking some rooms off by shutting doors or putting up baby gates. If possible, you can simply close the curtains to block her view. If you allow your puppy to keep engaging in this behavior, it will become a strong habit.

Also, redirect your puppy's attention with food-stuffed rubber toys or chew bones. Help to make the inside of your home more interesting to your puppy than what's going on outside.

Barking While Outside

If your puppy is outside all day, she probably is bored. A bored puppy often will bark at neighbors or passersby. It doesn't matter how many toys she has; if she's had them for a while, they will grow familiar to her. Rotate her toys every week so that they will seem new. Also, increase her exercise. Being alone in a fenced-in yard is usually not enough exercise for a puppy. She will likely run around for a bit, then lie down, and wait for something interesting to happen.

Invite your neighbors over for your puppy to meet. Give them treats to give your puppy. (However, don't force her if she is afraid of them and doesn't want to go near them.) If she's familiar with them, she will be less likely to bark in alarm when they come outside.

If your puppy is barking through the fence at another dog, and the other dog is barking back, it's best to separate them. You may think that she's being friendly, but she could be developing a behavior called "fence fighting." She could be challenging (or answering a challenge) from across the fence. This isn't good play behavior. It's preferable to teach your puppy how to play with other dogs without barking. Set up puppy play dates with other safe, well-behaved dogs in your area.

Also, consider bringing your puppy inside. If you crate train her, she can't destroy your home while you're away at work. She'll also be safer indoors. Many puppies have been stolen from backyards, and they also can learn how to dig out or jump fences out of boredom. You can help to prevent all these behaviors by keeping your puppy indoors while you're away from home.

Puppies bark for a variety of reasons, including because they are bored, protective, or afraid.

Barking at People or Other Dogs

If your puppy barks or growls at other people or dogs when you're out for a walk, she may be trying to tell you that she's afraid of them. You may notice that her ears are down, her tail tucked, and that she is trying to hide behind you. Some puppies, especially those who don't usually get to see or play with other puppies or people outside your family, may get overly excited when they see people or other dogs. They may bark, growl, and lunge on the leash toward them.

If your puppy does this, contact a professional, reward-based dog trainer to assist you. It also may be a good idea to put your puppy in kindergarten or a manners class to get her more socialized. Depending on the severity of the behavior, it may be better to start with private lessons. Never force a puppy to confront something she fears, because this can make the fear much worse. And if your puppy is acting aggressively, don't let her go up to the other dog to "let her see that everything's okay." The other dog may not appreciate your puppy's behavior and may react accordingly.

The Mouth Is Connected to . . . the Legs?

If your puppy is shooting off at the mouth too much, there's a good chance that it's because her legs are not in motion enough. Many puppies don't get enough exercise for their age and breed (or breed combination). If she is getting plenty of play breaks and exercise time, she won't feel as bored. She also will have less energy to spare for barking.

Barking to Get Something

You may have accidentally taught your puppy that, if she barks, she gets something. For example, she barks at you constantly while you're preparing her dinner. When you give her the food bowl, she gets quiet to eat. You've just rewarded her barking. Here's another example: She drops a toy in your lap and barks at you to throw it. If you throw it, you've paid her for barking. You have to change your habits before you can change your puppy's habits. First, stop giving any kind of attention or reward for barking.

The next time that your puppy barks to get something, give your *quiet* cue and freeze. Do absolutely nothing. She will become confused and may start barking more. Still freeze. Don't repeat the *quiet* cue over and over, don't lecture her, don't look her in the eyes (that's attention), and don't say anything. She will eventually stop. The second she does, mark "Yes" and continue what you were originally doing. She'll bark again. Repeat. If you are very clear—you move when she's quiet and not when she's barking—she'll learn that being quiet gets her closer to what she wants.

For example, let's say that she's brought you a ball to fetch, and she starts to bark. Tell her "Hush" (or whatever cue you've chosen) and freeze. The second she stops, mark "Yes!" and start to reach for the ball. She'll likely bark. Tell her "Hush" and freeze again. Only move toward throwing the ball for her when she's quiet. She really wants you to throw that ball. So, if you're clear in your communication, she will learn that her talking gets no action.

Barking in a Crate

Some puppies bark or whine when they're in their crates. This can be because they're not used to them yet. Don't yell at your puppy, because she can interpret that as attention. The best thing to do, although it can be the hardest thing to do, is to ignore it. If you let your puppy out of the crate when she is barking or crying, she will learn that all she has to do is bark or cry to get what she wants. And this is not a lesson that you want to teach her.

If you are following a proper crate program, your puppy is not being hurt in her crate. Be sure that you are making her crate a pleasant place by always giving her a treat for going in and by giving her some safe toys to enjoy as well. Also, give her plenty of potty breaks and lots of exercise outside her crate.

You may want to consider putting the crate in a different place.

In general, puppies prefer to be near you. This may mean putting up with barking and crying for a couple of sleepless nights if she still continues that behavior. But you can do it! Ignore it now, and there will be relief in the long run. Don't be tempted to lie down by her crate, let her out, or reassure her. If you do any of these things, you're teaching her that being noisy works, and you could be setting back your housetraining program and other training as well. If your puppy is too young to be unsupervised at night, and you let her out of the crate too early because she's barking, you are giving her the chance to eliminate inside the house. This is setting her up to fail. You may have a quiet night, but now you have housetraining accidents to deal with.

Instead, work on your crate training program more, and reward your puppy for quiet behavior in the crate. Stick with the program, and she will learn that the crate is a safe, cozy den.

If your puppy stays outside all day and tends to bark, she is probably bored.

What Not to Do

Avoid these common mistakes when trying to get your puppy to stop barking:

- **Yelling at her.** Shouting "No!" or "Hush!" or "Shut up!" is not likely to stop your puppy from barking. Instead, she could interpret this as you joining in her announcement, and it could encourage her to bark more. You may have noticed that when one dog in your neighborhood starts barking, other dogs chime in. It's a social behavior. If you yell at your puppy when she's barking, she interprets that as you joining in the discussion, just like the other dogs in your area.

- **Rewarding her for barking.** You may not think that you're rewarding your puppy for this behavior, but you may be giving her a paycheck without realizing it. For example, if she barks while you're eating dinner, and you give her a chew toy to keep her quiet, you've just paid her for barking. If she barks to be let out of her crate, and you open the door, you've paid her for barking. If she's outside and barks at you to let her in, and you do, you've paid her for barking. If you continue to do this, the barking will never go away because your puppy has learned that it works.

- **Having unrealistic expectations.** You may want your puppy to bark when someone comes to the door, but how long? How much barking is too much? Your puppy will not know unless you teach her what you want. Some people want their puppies only to bark when "bad" people approach. But if you can't tell the good guys from the bad ones, is it realistic to expect your puppy to determine who's who? You may have a puppy who has an instinct for judging people, but you also could have a puppy who'd happily greet a serial killer and offer him a tennis ball.

- **Not meeting her physical and mental needs.** If your puppy is outside in the backyard all day, she likely will grow bored and frustrated. If she's in her crate for too long without an appropriate number of potty or play breaks, she'll probably become bored and restless. If she's not getting the amount of exercise she needs for her breed and age, likely she'll become agitated and hyper. All these conditions can lead to excessive barking.

Common Problem Behaviors

Some common puppy problem behaviors include:

- barking
- coprophagia
- digging
- jumping up
- mouthing

COPROPHAGIA (EATING FECES)

Puppies usually love the taste of feces. It's unappetizing but true. They'll eat their own poop. If you have other dogs, they'll eat their feces, too. Horse manure can be especially tempting. And if you have a cat, well, cat poop is a delicacy to your puppy! The habit of eating stools is called *coprophagia*.

Not every puppy develops this habit. But if your puppy is eating poop, it's a bigger problem than just bad breath and nasty puppy kisses. She could ingest intestinal parasites and get sick. Puppies who eat large amounts of horse manure can develop severe diarrhea and vomiting.

Usually, puppies who develop coprophagia are not suffering from any nutritional deficiencies. In other words, there's nothing missing in their diets that causes them to crave poop. They can develop the habit out of boredom, from being raised in close confinement that isn't properly cleaned, or because of something as simple as they tried it one day and liked the taste.

What to Do

There are theories about adding things to your puppy's diet to make the taste of her poop less appealing. You can purchase these products from pet stores or your veterinarian. You also may have heard about adding things to her food, from meat tenderizer to pineapple to pumpkin. Some people experience success with these items; others have no success at all.

A surefire way to solve the problem is through good management. As soon as your puppy eliminates, pick it up and deposit it in a waste receptacle out of her reach. If you have other dogs, pick up after them right away, too. Put your litter box in a place where your cat can access it but your puppy can't. If you are around horses, keep your puppy on leash and make sure that she does not get near any horse manure. If she never has access to poop, she can't eat it and thus can't get sick from it. It may be a bit more work to clean up after your puppy promptly, but it's healthier for everyone in your family.

Some dogs crave stool for a few rare medical reasons. If you have concerns, always check with your veterinarian.

What Not to Do

Never rub your puppy's nose in her stool or scream at her for eating her poop. Yes, it's a disgusting habit—to you, not to your puppy. She thinks it's delicious! Just manage the issue and train her to leave her stools alone.

DIGGING

Some puppies are like four-legged bulldozers. Why do dogs like to dig?

- **Some breeds are more prone than others.** Terriers, especially, have been bred to dig up vermin and kill them. So, your terrier puppy is just exercising her genetic right to unearth invading critters.
- **They're warm or cold.** Digging a hole provides a warm spot in the winter and a cool spot in the summer.
- **They smell something down there.** Dogs have keen senses of smell. If there's something underground that's caught their interest, they may be inspired to dig it up.
- **They're good at it.** Look at those paws. They were meant to dig!

What to Do

To teach your puppy not to dig, you have to be present to catch her in the act. It doesn't do any good to reprimand her for holes she dug while you were at work. If your puppy is a digger, confine her in the house when you are away instead of giving her opportunities to practice digging behaviors outside.

One way to deal with digging is through management. Purchase some inexpensive low fencing, available in the gardening center of your local department or home improvement store. Use the fencing to set up a designated "dig pit" in your yard. Set up a square of your yard with an opening for your puppy to exit and enter. Fill it with sand or loose dirt, and hide some toys in there for your puppy to find. This allows her to pursue her natural digging behavior in a spot that is acceptable to you. The fencing gives her clear boundaries.

Teach your puppy to dig in her dig pit. Take her to it and start digging, and encourage her to join you. When she does, mark "Yes!" and praise her. If you catch her digging outside the area, use a stern voice, say "No!", and

Digging is a natural dog behavior.

gently take her collar. Run over to the dig pit with your puppy (don't drag her) and encourage her to dig in her designated area. When she does, mark "Yes!" and praise her. Be specific—you don't like it when she digs in one place, and you love it when she digs in her dig pit. Make sure that you are consistent, and never let her have a chance to practice digging outside her designated spot when you can't watch her. Giving your puppy her own dig pit is a nice compromise between acknowledging your puppy's natural instincts and your need for a nice landscape.

If your puppy enjoys digging in your flowers, set up a separate area of your yard for her to dig to her heart's content.

Some people would prefer that their puppies not dig at all. Again, to stop digging completely, you must be there to address the behavior when it happens, or your puppy cannot learn what you want. When you witness her digging, simply use a verbal "No!" and redirect her behavior toward a toy, chew bone, game of fetch, or other activity. The second she engages in the preferred activity, mark "Yes!" and praise her. Every time you catch her digging repeat. By being specific that you do not approve of her digging but love it when she engages in other activities, she can learn what you want. It may take several repetitions for your puppy to understand; this is normal. It will take more repetitions if she already has developed the habit of digging in your yard.

You can purchase dig-deterrent chemicals, but the results can be spotty. With the sprays, especially, you may have to make frequent, repeated treatments of your lawn because of humidity, rain, or other weather conditions. Instead of spending money on those, try filling the hole almost all the way up to the top with dirt. Put some of your puppy's poop in the hole, then cover with a thin layer of dirt. For some reason, many puppies don't like to dig near their stools.

If your puppy is digging out of your yard completely, you have a serious problem. She could get hit by a car, encounter dangerous dogs or wildlife, or even run across some unpleasant people who could hurt her. There also are leash laws in many places, and you could incur fees if your puppy is caught by animal control. Puppies who dig out of yards are usually bored. Other frequent escapees are male puppies who are not yet neutered and who are following their hormones.

When your puppy runs around the neighborhood, it's very exciting, so she learns that being outside the yard is much more fun than being inside. This is a sad lesson, because you want your puppy to think that her home is the best place. If she is digging out (or jumping out) of your yard, confine her inside for her safety. Crate training your puppy will help to keep your home intact and your puppy much safer than she would be roaming the neighborhood.

What Not to Do

- **Don't push your puppy's nose in the hole.** She will have no idea what you are upset about. Instead of teaching her not to dig a hole, you could be teaching her to be afraid of you.
- **Don't let your puppy watch you plant things.** If you have a digger puppy, she may want to help you with your gardening. Put her in the house when you do any planting or digging in your yard so that she can't observe you and try to join in.

JUMPING UP

Puppies usually jump up because they want your attention and because you give it to them. Of course, if your puppy jumps up on you and you laugh and pet her, you're teaching her to jump up on you. Puppies do what works. If it pays to keep jumping on you, they'll keep doing it. Some paychecks can be subtle:

- If you're watching television and your puppy puts her front paws on your legs and you scratch her ears, you're paying her for jumping up.
- If your puppy jumps up on you and you push her away, you're paying her for jumping up. You've given her physical attention. She interprets this as petting or part of the game.
- If your puppy jumps on you and you scold her, you're paying her for jumping up. You've given her verbal attention. Whether

you think the attention is negative or positive, it's still attention to your puppy.

What to Do

Before you can fix your puppy's behavior, change your own. Or maybe you aren't paying your puppy for jumping, but your friends or family are. That can be a more difficult challenge—to fix their behavior, too! If one person rewards your puppy for jumping but others don't, your puppy will have a difficult time learning not to jump on people. Everyone should be consistent teachers so that your puppy has consistent lessons.

STEP 1:

a) Have a treat hidden in your hand. Jump around and act excited—in other words, set the situation up so that your puppy will likely jump up on you.

b) The second your puppy jumps up on you, stop moving. Turn your head slightly away, and fold your arms across your chest. Act as if you are completely ignoring her, but it's important that you can still see her. Otherwise, you will not be able to accurately mark the behavior that you want, which is her getting off you. So don't turn completely around with your back to your puppy, or you won't be able to see her.

c) Give the cue "Off." Do not use a mean voice! This is information, not discipline. Your puppy does not have a clue what this word means yet. Be sure to use the same cue each time. For example, if you want to use the cue "Get down" for this, don't also use "Down" to mean lie down, too.

STEP 2:

a) Continue to ignore your puppy. Don't talk to her, don't look in her eyes, and don't lecture her. Do nothing. Don't be tempted to use the treat to lure her off you. This would be like doing her homework for her. You want her to learn this on her own, without a temptation to lure her away. You may not always have a treat with you when she jumps on you. Just ignore her. Remember, she wants your attention. If you don't give her any, she will get off, because jumping up isn't paying her.

b) The second your puppy has all four paws on the ground, mark "Yes!" and give her the treat that you had hidden in your hand. Don't wait for her to sit—just mark the very second she has four paws on the floor. She may eventually sit for your

Puppies usually jump up because they want attention. If they get it, they'll continue to jump.

attention, but if you wait for that, she won't associate getting off you with the cue "Off," because too much time will have elapsed.

Troubleshooting: What if your puppy jumps up to get the treat? Don't give it to her. Pull the treat back and wait for her to get all four paws on the floor.

What if your puppy is too fast? If she jumps, and you've barely gotten "Off" out of your mouth before she's off you and jumping up again, try to be faster than your puppy. Some puppies, especially smaller breeds, are like pogo sticks! Stick with it, and try to accurately mark the behavior when she has all four paws on the floor.

Jumping Up: Next Steps

Once you have taught your puppy to stop jumping on you, it's time to teach her not to jump on your guests. After all, your friends and family may not appreciate being mauled every time they come to visit. Two exercises will help with this behavior: Greeting Manners and Sitting Politely for Petting.

You will need another person to help you. Be sure to instruct them not to reward your puppy in any way for jumping up. Explain to them that this includes laughing, giggling, petting, and even looking at your puppy. Your puppy thinks that any attention is good attention!

Greeting Manners

STEP 1:

a) Stand inside your house. Have a treat hidden in your hand. Put your puppy on leash so that you can better control your environment. You won't use the leash to correct her, just to prevent her from running off and getting distracted.

b) Your friend or family member is outside. Have him ring the doorbell.

c) Answer the door and greet your friend. Your puppy will likely jump on the person.

STEP 2:

a) The second your puppy makes contact with the "guest," give the cue "Off." Your guest should turn away from your puppy and fold his arms across his chest. He should completely ignore your puppy.

b) Both of you wait. Don't lure her off with the treat, and don't keep repeating, "Off! Off! Off!" Just wait. She will realize that she's not getting any attention from your guest, and she will get off.

STEP 3:

a) The second that your puppy puts all four paws on the ground, mark "Yes!" and give her the treat from your hand.

b) Have your guest attempt to pet your puppy and give her the attention that she wants. If she jumps up again, immediately repeat Step 2. Your puppy should only get attention when all four paws are on the floor.

To stop your puppy from jumping up, teach the sit as an alternative behavior.

c) Repeat from Step 1 several times more, then take a break until your next training session. If you are consistent about practicing this exercise at the door, your puppy will learn that she only gets attention when she's off your guests, not on them.

Sitting Politely for Petting

STEP 1:

a) Have several treats in your hand. Give the cue "Sit." As soon as your puppy sits, mark "Yes!" and give her a treat.

b) Your friend should approach your puppy. Before she can get up to greet him, mark "Yes!" and give her another treat.

c) Your friend should reach under your puppy's chin for her to sniff his hand, then pet her. Mark "Yes!" and give her a treat as long as her rear end remains on the ground.

d) As long as your puppy remains in a sit, give her an occasional "Yes!" and a treat.

STEP 2:

a) If your puppy gets up, your friend should immediately fold his arms across his chest and look away from your puppy. He should completely ignore her.

b) Don't repeat the *sit* cue. Instead, use your hand signal to lure her into a sit. As soon as she sits again, mark "Yes" and give her a treat. Your friend should start petting your puppy again.

c) As long as your puppy is sitting, give her treats and attention. When she's not sitting, give her neither. She will learn that all she has to do is to sit to get the good stuff.

d) Give your puppy the release cue "Okay!"

Troubleshooting: What if your puppy keeps getting up over and over? Go back to practicing the *sit* cue without the petting part; she may need more practice. Be sure that you are not rewarding her for getting up before you give your release cue. Remember, rewards to your puppy can be you saying, "Sit! Sit! Sit!" over and over again, because that's attention. Also, shorten the amount of time that you're expecting her to sit still and be petted. You may be asking too much of her at this point.

What Not to Do

Do not knee your puppy in the chest or pinch her toes or use any other kind of physical punishment if she jumps on you. This can backfire. You may teach her not to jump on you, but she'll probably still jump on a child, senior citizen, or anyone else who can't use strong force to stop her. Or you'll teach her to be afraid of you. Instead, use the lessons in this section so that everyone in your family can benefit.

If you have a shy or fearful puppy, do not make her sit for petting. You may be asking too much of her to expect her to sit still while what she perceives as a monster approaches her. She may be so frightened that she snaps or growls. If you have a shy puppy, work with a professional trainer to help her overcome her fearfulness.

MOUTHING

Puppies have sharp needle teeth, and it hurts when they chew on you. There will be times when you probably feel that your puppy thinks of you as a two-legged chew toy. Why does she do that? Is your puppy being dominant? Is she trying to show you that

Good Things Come to Those Who Sit

If you only allow your puppy to be petted when she's sitting, she'll learn that that's how she gets attention. You will end up with a puppy who goes up to people and sits. This is a lovely behavior, because a puppy who is sitting is not jumping up or knocking people over. Make sure that all your friends, family, and even strangers only pet your puppy when she's politely sitting. She'll make a great greeting impression!

she's boss? Not at all.

Have you ever seen two puppies or older dogs playing together? They mouth each other as part of the game—that's how they play. When your puppy mouths you, she's trying to engage you in the same kind of play. But our skin is a lot more fragile than a puppy's skin. Some people, such as children or seniors, have even more delicate skin. If a puppy mouths them, they could easily get bruised or cut.

Although mouthing is a normal puppy behavior, you must teach her bite inhibition before her teeth harm someone.

Your puppy will not mean to hurt anyone—she's just playing. She doesn't have any idea of the damage that those needle teeth can do. It's up to you to teach her that mouthing is not an acceptable behavior, and it's important to teach this now, before she grows up to be an adult dog who mouths people.

What to Do

If your puppy mouths you, teach her "bite inhibition." Bite inhibition is the concept that puppies shouldn't bite down hard on people. You want her to stop using humans as her chew toys, and you want to teach her how to be careful with her teeth.

STEP 1:

a) When your puppy mouths you, yelp "Ouch!" It's important to yelp like you're wounded, not like you're angry. Act like you're really in pain.

b) Immediately turn away from your puppy and completely ignore her for 10 to 15 seconds. Don't lecture her, don't look at her, and don't even acknowledge her. This will teach your puppy that mouthing makes her lose the attention of her best friend.

c) Remember, your puppy is not trying to hurt you—she's trying to play. Once you yelp, she's likely to stop and look at you to see if you're okay or even to apologize. Keep ignoring her for the full time so that she learns that her teeth made you quit the game.

STEP 2:

a) Turn back around. Find the nearest toy that your puppy is allowed to have and immediately offer it to her.

b) When she takes the toy, mark "Yes!" and praise her.

Repeat these steps every time your puppy mouths you. She will learn that she gets your attention and affection only if her teeth don't make contact. The second she mouths you, yelp and ignore her. Be consistent with your lessons. If you let her get away with it sometimes but not others, the behavior will worsen. She will not learn that mouthing is inappropriate. If you are consistent, and everyone who comes in contact with your puppy follows the same routine, your puppy will one day start to mouth you and think better of it. This is cause for celebration!

Troubleshooting: What if your puppy gets all riled up when you yelp? Some puppies get a little crazy when they hear an "Ouch!" For these puppies, try a softer whine, like "Owwwwwww." Make sure that you're acting hurt and that your yelp doesn't sound so excited that your puppy interprets it as part of the game.

What if your puppy starts biting at your pants leg or jumping up on you while you're ignoring her? Some puppies may get frustrated when you ignore them, so they try to engage your attention the only way that they know how: by pestering you. Perhaps

The Difference Between Mouthing and Biting

Mouthing is normal behavior for a puppy. However, some puppy owners worry that, instead of having a mouthing issue, they really have an aggression issue. How can you tell the difference? Here are some signs that you may be dealing with something more serious than normal puppy mouthing.

• If your puppy growls, snaps, or bites you when you reach for her food bowl.

• If your puppy growls, snaps, or bites you when you try to take a toy away from her. This also may occur only with toys that your puppy finds to be of high value. For example, she may willingly give up a tennis ball but growl when you try to take away a pig's ear or rawhide chew.

• If your puppy growls, snaps, or bites you when you try to get her off the furniture.

• If your puppy growls, snaps, or bites you when you try to pick her up.

If your puppy does any of these things, seek the assistance of a professional dog trainer or applied animal behaviorist. This behavior will not get better on its own; in fact, it could get much worse.

Early, consistent training may help to prevent some problem behaviors.

this has worked for them in the past. Maybe they kept jumping and clawing and nipping until they finally got a reaction. It's important not to reward this behavior. Remember, any attention can be interpreted as good attention by a puppy! You shouldn't have to get hurt, however. If your puppy is so frantic that she practically attacks you if you ignore her, leave the room if necessary. Don't leave her for long, because she shouldn't be unattended. Return in 10 to 15 seconds and try again. You also can give her a quick time-out in her crate. Be sure that this puppy is getting plenty of exercise for her breed and age. Puppies who aren't getting their daily exercise requirements can sometimes act this way. If the problem persists, call a professional reward-based dog trainer to observe and assist you.

What Not to Do

You may be tempted to use physical punishment with your puppy if she mouths you. This can backfire. Because your puppy is most likely trying to play with you, she's liable to think that you've figured out the game if you get physical with her. She'll come back at you harder. You also might teach her to only keep her teeth off the loudest or strongest person in the house. You don't want her to

When To Call a Professional

If you have a problem with plumbing, you call a plumber. If you have a problem with your car, you call a mechanic. Don't hesitate to call a professional dog trainer if you think you need help. How do you know it's time?

- *Before* you reach the end of your rope. If you're getting increasingly frustrated with your puppy's behavior, get help before you reach a boiling point. If you wait too long, you won't be willing to put forth the effort it will take to fix her behavior because you'll be too frustrated. Be proactive.

- If your puppy is shy or fearful. These puppies need extra help so that their shyness does not become worse.

- If your puppy is aggressive. These puppies also need extra help before they grow bigger and cause more damage. Aggressive dogs are also a tremendous liability. If your puppy is growling, snapping, or biting, the problem will not go away by itself. Get help now.

Before choosing a trainer, do your research. You can contact the Association of Pet Dog Trainers (APDT) at www.apdt.com or the Certification Council for Professional Dog Trainers (CCPDT) at www.ccpdt.org for trainers in your area. Interview the trainer carefully and ask for references. Make sure that she uses modern, science-based training methods and will not cause harm to your puppy with harsh techniques or tools.

If your puppy has a severe issue, such as fearfulness or aggression, your veterinarian may refer you to a certified applied animal behaviorist. These are specialists with specific education in animal behavior, certified by the Animal Behavior Society (ABS). You'll find more information at www.animalbehavior.org.

mouth *anyone* in your household. If your puppy mouths you:
- Don't yell at her.
- Don't "pop" her under the chin or grab her by the scruff.
- Don't grab her tongue or stick your fingers down her throat.
- Don't spank her.
- Don't flip her upside down (the old-fashioned "alpha roll").

All these things could make the problem worse.

SHYNESS AND FEARFULNESS

Some puppies are born shy or fearful. They may have had timid parents. Temperament is passed down from parent to puppy, so if your puppy's parents were shy, there's a good chance that it's in her genes. Some puppies are shy or fearful because they haven't had a lot of positive social experiences during their first 16 weeks of life. Maybe they never left the house or kennel except to go to the veterinarian. Or maybe they were "outside" puppies who never enjoyed diverse interactions.

Shy puppies can be very challenging and frustrating. You want to make them less afraid of the world. You may want to do things with your puppy that require you to take her places or require that she be friendly with strangers. Unfortunately, you can't reason with a shy puppy and simply explain to her that there's no reason to be afraid. Instead, you must be very patient and help her overcome her fears.

What to Do

If you have a shy puppy, it's best to contact a professional reward-based trainer to assist you. She will personally evaluate your puppy and help to develop a treatment plan to build her confidence.

What Not to Do

In the meantime, avoid these common mistakes:

If you have a shy puppy, contact a professional reward-based trainer to assist you.

- **Forcing your shy puppy to confront her fears.** Never put your puppy in someone's lap if she has shown fear toward that person or has been hesitant to approach him. Never pull your puppy on leash toward an object that she is afraid of, and never discipline her for being afraid. All these actions are likely to increase her fear and could make her distrust you. Shy puppies always should set their own pace for overcoming their fears.
- **Rewarding your puppy for shy behavior.** If your puppy is trembling, and you scoop her up and fuss over her, you actually could make her fear worse. She may think that if you're this upset, then she must have something to worry about. You're also praising her for behavior that you don't want. Resist the urge to coddle your puppy. Instead, act very confident and casual so that she can learn that there's nothing for her to worry about.

Most of the problem behaviors that drive us crazy are quite normal for growing puppies. If your puppy has a problem behavior, it doesn't mean that she is bad or a horrible pet. It just means that you have to better communicate with her what you want her to understand. Be patient, and if necessary, get professional help. Nip problems in the bud now so that they don't become ingrained lifetime habits.

7

ACTIVITIES

With Your Puppy

M any breeds have a long history of being bred for a specific job. If you chose a Border Collie puppy, for instance, you have a very active puppy on your hands. If you don't have sheep for your puppy to expend her genetic energy on, you need to come up with another job for her to do. Sporting breeds, such as Labrador Retrievers and Golden Retrievers, also were bred for a job. If you don't hunt, you need to find something else for them to do, or they can become hyperactive and destructive. High-energy puppies benefit from energetic activities that the two of you can share.

However, don't think that you have to have a high-energy breed to have fun with your puppy. Lower-key puppies can enjoy plenty of activities, too. Also, although some registries only allow purebred dogs to participate, others allow mixed-breed puppies to join in the fun.

After trying an activity with your puppy, you may find that she doesn't seem well suited for it. Or she may not have the build or robust strength for a certain sport. Not all of us are athletes. Not everyone loves outdoor activities. Not all puppies are suited for different activities, and this is perfectly okay. Don't force your puppy to participate in something that she doesn't enjoy. These activities are supposed to be fun for you two to share, so resist the temptation to put your competitive spirit ahead of your puppy's welfare. There are plenty of other opportunities for you to share with your puppy. And she's already a pro at her most important activity—being your family companion.

COMPETITIVE SPORTS

If you're a sports fan, there is a variety of sports that you can enjoy with your puppy. Whether you seek the thrill of winning or just want to exercise and have fun with your companion, there's plenty to do together!

Agility is a sport in which a dog must navigate a timed obstacle course.

Agility

Agility is a sport in which a dog is judged running through a timed obstacle course. The course has jumps, poles that she must weave in and out of, tunnels, and other obstacles. It's great exercise for an active dog and for you, too! Participating in agility also can boost the confidence of shy dogs.

Dogs can earn titles by completing courses under specific requirements. There are different levels of difficulty. Once you and your dog have earned a title in one level, you can advance to the next level. There are different height classes, and the obstacles are set appropriately for each height class. This is for safety reasons— you wouldn't want a Chihuahua to have to go over the same size jump as an Irish Wolfhound. There are also different types of agility competitions. For example, the American Kennel Club (AKC) offers a Standard class, which has certain obstacles, and a Jumpers with Weaves class, which only has jumps, tunnels, and weave poles.

Agility is regulated by dog registries. The AKC offers agility competition for purebred dogs. The United Kennel Club (UKC), the North American Dog Agility Council (NADAC), the United States Dog Agility Association (USDAA), and the Australian Shepherd

Club of America (ASCA) also offer agility competition, and all of them offer agility to mixed-breed dogs.

To participate safely in agility, your puppy should get a clearance from her veterinarian. This is a very athletic sport, so you want to make sure that her body is sound enough to participate. She can begin to learn some agility obstacles at a young age, but she should wait until her bones are mature before you teach her any of the jumps.

How to Get Started

- Get your puppy a full veterinary checkup and explain to your veterinarian that you would like her to participate in agility.
- Visit a local agility trial. Agility is a great spectator sport. It's exciting to watch the dogs run through the course, and you can get an idea of how the competition is run.
- Join your local agility club. Some local obedience clubs do both obedience and agility. Volunteer to help at a local agility trial for an insider's look at how a trial operates.
- Read books about agility. It's also helpful to watch training videos so that you can see the sport in action.

Dog Shows (Conformation)

Conformation is the sport in which purebred dogs are judged based on their breed standard. You may have seen these events on television, where the dogs parade around a ring. The shows are regulated by a registering body. The largest dog registry in the United States is the AKC. Each AKC breed has a parent club that dictates the breed standard. The standard explains the requirements for coat color, size, structure, movement, temperament—every detail pertaining to a particular breed of dog. Individual dogs are judged based on how closely they meet their breed standard. First, they compete with others of their breed. Winners of that round go on to compete against other dogs in their group (herding, terrier, sporting, non-sporting, working, hound, toy). Winners of that group go on to compete for Best in Show.

Dogs who win are awarded points. After accumulating a certain number of points under specific conditions, a dog can earn the title of Champion. These dogs will have a "Ch" in front of their names, such as "Ch. Anderson's Pride 'n' Joy."

The Waiting Game

Some activities may have to wait until your puppy has had all her shots, like those activities that require that you go out in public places. Some may have to wait until her body is more mature and stronger, such as some of the active, sporting activities.

In conformation competition, a dog is judged against the standard of the breed.

The goal of conformation is to preserve the integrity of a breed by promoting the best breeding stock. For this reason, only dogs who are not neutered can participate. Puppies as young as six months of age can enter a dog show.

How to Get Started

- Join your local kennel club. You can get a great deal of information from people who are active in the sport, and they can help to evaluate your puppy's potential.
- Visit dog shows in your area. If your puppy is not entered, you cannot bring her to the show. But you'll enjoy seeing all the different breeds of dogs, and you'll be able to see others of your puppy's breed and get an idea of how the process works.
- Read books about dog shows. If you've never been to a dog show, it can be a bit bewildering. People are running around with numbered armbands, going in and out of rings, and frantically grooming their dogs—it can be hard to figure out who's headed where and why. Read up on things ahead of time, and you'll have a better understanding of what's going on.

Flyball

Flyball is a team relay race competition. Four dogs participate on each team. Each dog leaps over hurdles in a lane, and when she reaches the end, steps on a spring-loaded box that launches a ball. She catches the ball and races back over the hurdles. When she crosses the starting line, the next dog on the team takes off. Dogs can earn titles by accumulating points based on their team's speed, with specific requirements. Flyball is regulated by the North American Flyball Association (NAFA).

Flyball is a great sport for active dogs, especially those who love balls. Although you can teach your puppy to fetch at a young age, you'll need to wait to participate in flyball until after her bones mature because of the jumping requirements.

How to Get Started

- Get your puppy a full veterinary checkup and explain to your veterinarian that you would like her to participate in flyball.
- Attend a local flyball event. It's a great spectator sport!

Flying Disc

Flying disc is a competition in which dogs are judged on how well they catch a flying disc. Some competitions award points for speed, stunts, or even navigating obstacles. It's a great sport for active dogs. Competition is regulated by organizations including the International Disc Dog Handlers Association (IDDHA) and the Flying Disc Dog Organization (FDDO).

To participate in flying disc, your puppy should have a thorough veterinary checkup. This is a very athletic sport, and you must make sure that your puppy's body is sound and healthy enough to participate. Although you can familiarize your puppy with a flying disc from a very young age, you should not participate in the sport until she is grown and her bones are mature. The high leaps that dogs achieve to catch the disc require strong spines, hips, knees, and legs for safe landings.

How to Get Started

- Get your puppy a full veterinary checkup and explain to your veterinarian that you would like her to participate in flying disc.

You can familiarize your puppy with a flying disc from a young age, but wait to participate until she is grown and her bones are mature.

• Attend a local flying disc competition. These are more popular in some areas of the country than others, so you may have to look to find one.

Obedience

Obedience is a sport in which a dog is judged on her ability to perform a certain set of exercises. Dogs can earn titles by earning passing scores under specific requirements. There are different levels of difficulty. Once a dog and handler earn a title in one level, they can advance to the next level. The sport is regulated by a dog registry. The AKC runs dog obedience competition for purebred dogs, but there are also other registries, such as the United Kennel Club (UKC), that allow mixed-breed dogs to participate.

Puppies as young as six months of age can enter obedience competition, and neutered puppies are also eligible.

How to Get Started

• Train your puppy. Take her to a puppy kindergarten or other reward-based group class.
• Visit obedience trials in your area. You can see all the different levels of competition and become familiar with the different exercises for each level.
• Join your local obedience club. You'll get tips from people who are active in the sport. You also can volunteer to help with its local obedience trial. By volunteering, you can get a great insider's look as to how the sport works.
• Read books about dog obedience competition. The more that you understand the sport, the better you can enjoy it.

Rally

Rally is a sport in which dog and handler teams compete by following a course of signs in a ring. Each of the signs has a specific exercise that the team completes before moving on to the next sign. Unlike traditional obedience, which is more formal, rally encourages owners to talk to their dogs throughout the competition.

Rally is regulated by registries. The first registry to launch rally in the United States was the Association of Pet Dog Trainers (APDT). APDT rally allows purebred dogs, mixed-breed dogs, and even dogs with disabilities to participate. You can use food treats in the ring, and there is a category for children to participate in as well. The AKC also offers rally for purebred dogs.

Dogs can earn titles by earning qualified scores under specific requirements. There are different levels of competition. Once a team earns a title at one level, it can move on to the next level.

You can start rally training your puppy at a very young age, but she will have to wait until she is six months old to compete in a rally trial.

How to Get Started

- Visit a local rally trial. Rally is one of the newer sports, so it may not have come to your area yet. But because it emphasizes fun and is less formal than traditional obedience, it is growing in popularity.
- Attend a rally class. Rally classes also are growing in popularity. Some local obedience clubs do both obedience and rally. Even if you don't have a rally-specific class in your area, take your puppy to a reward-based group class. You'll see a lot of the exercises that you'll learn in a regular group class on rally signs in the ring.
- Read books about rally.

FUN STUFF TO DO WITH YOUR PUPPY

Not everyone enjoys sports, but that doesn't mean that you can't have fun with your puppy. From playing a simple game of fetch to learning how best to travel with your puppy, you can participate in a variety of activities together.

Fetch is a fun exercise to play with your puppy.

Fetch

Playing fetch is a great, fun exercise to play with your puppy. It also can be very useful when she learns to bring you specific objects, and it can help to prevent destructive behavior. For example, if your puppy learns to bring you an object, she's not taking it somewhere and chewing it to bits.

Some puppies are born retrievers. Some breeds are also genetically inclined for the activity. But even some Labrador Retriever puppies can act like they've never heard of fetching before. If you want your puppy to play a good game of fetch, you have to teach her.

What to Do
STEP 1:

First, teach your puppy the *take it* and *drop it* cues from Chapter 5.

a) Have treats handy. Find a toy that your puppy just loves. Instead of offering her the toy to take from your hands, set it on the ground. Give the cue "Take it." If she picks it up, mark "Yes!" and praise her. Then give the cue "Drop it." If she drops it, mark "Yes!" and give her a treat. If she doesn't pick it up, practice holding it for her two times, then try it on the floor again.

b) Gradually work toward longer times while your puppy holds the object before you mark "Yes." Try for three or four seconds. If you find that she's dropping the object before you mark "Yes," take it back a few seconds and work up more gradually. Your goal is to try to get her to hold the object for longer periods of time.

STEP 2:

When your puppy is reliably taking the toy off the ground and holding it, it's time to move on to this step.

a) Toss the toy up and down, and act excited until your puppy gets excited, too. Throw the toy a very short distance, and encourage your puppy to go after it.

b) If she runs after the toy, praise her.

c) When she reaches the toy, say "Take it." When she picks it up, mark "Yes" and praise her.

STEP 3:

a) Repeat Step 2. When your puppy takes the toy, move back a few steps and hold out your hand. Give her the cue "Fetch!" Use a friendly voice.

b) When she reaches you, give her the "Drop it" cue. If she drops it in your hand, mark "Yes" and give her a treat.

c) Gradually work up to longer distances. Keep training sessions short. If at any time the training session starts to break down, take a break. When you try again, break the training session into smaller steps.

STEP 4:

When your puppy is reliably fetching, you can use different items. Keep in mind that if you introduce a new item, you may have to start at the beginning with training the exercise. This is normal because the new item may confuse your puppy.

What Not to Do

If your puppy has something in her mouth, don't yell at her! This is a surefire way to teach her to go and hide the prize, where she'll destroy it or swallow it. You may never find it again.

Don't chase her, either. If you chase your puppy, she'll run away from you. That's not what you want to teach her. Instead, sit still. Hold out your hands and excitedly give her a cue, such as "Bring it!" or "Fetch!" Use a friendly voice. If she comes toward you, praise her. When she reaches you, say "Drop it" and mark "Yes"

Hiking and Camping Tips

- Be sure that your puppy is up to date on her flea and tick control medication. Check her frequently for ticks, burrs, foxtails, and the like.

- Bring your puppy first-aid kit. Check her paw pads frequently for cuts and scrapes. Watch how the weather is affecting her. Before your trip, get contact information for the nearest veterinarian and veterinary emergency clinic at your destination.

- Take plenty of rest stops, and watch for signs of overexertion or heatstroke.

- Always keep your puppy on leash. Do not leave her tethered and unsupervised, because she could get tangled around tent poles, tables, or trees.

- Always pick up after your puppy and dispose of her waste in a proper receptacle.

when she releases the item.

Hiking and Camping

If you enjoy hiking or camping, your puppy can be a great companion. Because you will be in public places where sick dogs may have been and where wildlife lives, your puppy must have all her shots before you take her hiking or camping. For camping alone, your puppy doesn't have to reach her full maturity, but if you want her to hike or carry a backpack, wait until her bones are mature, or you could cause her injury. As always, before any physical activity it's important to get your puppy a thorough veterinary checkup to ensure that she's in good health and is a good candidate for the activity. It's best to start out with short trips and gradually work up to longer ones to increase her stamina and gradually get her used to the exercise and experience.

Before camping or hiking with your puppy, make sure that you understand all the rules for the place you'll be visiting. Some trails and campsites do not allow dogs. Read books on how to hike or camp with your puppy so that you can learn more about what to expect and what problems and dangers to avoid.

Puppies who hike or camp must have excellent manners. They will be exposed to different people and be expected to behave themselves at campsites and not disturb your fellow campers. Teach your puppy to walk politely on leash, and make sure that she has plenty of positive socialization experiences so that she will be confident and friendly in new surroundings. Also, work on your housetraining so that she learns to potty on cue. You don't want to have to walk a long distance just waiting for your puppy to find the "perfect spot" to relieve herself. If she has a barking problem, work on that *before* your trip. Remember, your puppy will be experiencing different sights and sounds on the trail and in the campsite, so she may be tempted to bark, whine, or for certain breeds, howl. If you want your dog to carry a backpack, train her to do so *before* your trip. Be sure to work up to greater weights gradually.

If you find that your puppy has specific issues, like pulling on leash or barking at other campers, work on those issues at home and try the activity again. Always set your puppy up to succeed. For example, if you know that your puppy is hesitant around small children, do not let a small child pet her at a campsite. And never let a mob of kids surround her—you're just setting her up for disaster. Work with a reward-based trainer to help your puppy with this and any other issue so that she can learn to be a wonderful hiking and camping companion.

Your puppy will make a great companion on most family outings.

Jogging

If you're a jogger, you may enjoy sharing that activity with your puppy. Many high-energy puppies would love to run with you, but you should wait until their bones are mature before starting any strenuous running activity with them. If you begin this athletic activity too early, your puppy could sustain injuries.

Talk with your veterinarian to see if your puppy is a good candidate for jogging. She will need to be healthy, sound, and preferably not a flat-nosed breed, because they often have breathing difficulties.

When you do start, start slowly. Train your dog to run short distances, and gradually work up to longer ones. Always carry water with you for her to drink, keep a close eye for signs of overexertion and heatstroke, and be careful of the ground that you run on. It's hotter for a dog to run on asphalt because she doesn't have shoes to protect her feet. Check her paw pads regularly for cuts or scrapes.

Until your puppy is mature enough to jog with you, train her to

Packing for Your Puppy

What you bring for your puppy depends on where you're going and how long you'll be gone. But here are a few general items to remember to bring along:

1. **Water.** Your puppy should have easy access to water throughout your trip. Because water quality differs in different locations, bringing water from home could prevent an upset puppy stomach.

2. **Identification.** Make sure that your puppy wears her ID at all times. You also may want to get a temporary tag to put on her collar with the contact information for where you'll be staying.

3. **Crate.** She'll have a safe, familiar den to travel in the car and stay in once you reach your destination.

4. Treats. Use your travels as training opportunities for your puppy. Reward her good behavior as you go.

5. **Toys.** Bring a few chew toys to keep her occupied in the car and during your stay.

6. **Cleanup supplies.** Bring a few towels, some pet enzymatic cleaner, and baby wipes just in case messes occur.

7. **A copy of her health records.** Bring this if you are going out of town, even for a day. Should something happen, and you need to take your puppy to a local vet, he will find this information useful.

8. **First-aid kit.** This will come in handy in case of emergency.

NYLABONE

Make sure that your puppy is physically sound before participating in any sport or activity.

behave politely on leash and work on your socialization exercises. These will help you later, when she's ready to become your jogging partner.

Travel

Traveling with your puppy can be a fun adventure—or a nightmare if you're not prepared. Not all puppies take to car rides. Some are afraid or even become carsick. Others get so excited in the car that you think they'll explode. And what if you want to fly with your puppy? If you ever want to take your puppy places, you'll need to teach her how to be a good traveler.

Traveling by Car

If your puppy ever travels by car, she must be secured in a crate or wearing a canine seatbelt. Dogs should never be allowed to be loose in a car. They can get tangled up with you and cause an accident. Or if you're ever cut off in traffic and have to hit the brakes, they could be hurled about inside the vehicle or even thrown through the windshield. Just as you wear a seatbelt, your puppy should be kept safe and secure, too.

If you have a car that's small but you have a growing puppy, or if your puppy's crate is too awkward to move in and out of your vehicle, you still can keep her safe with a canine seatbelt. This is a harness that fits snugly onto your puppy, with a loop that secures to your car's seatbelt or to a bolt on your vehicle's floor.

Get a seatbelt that has padding for comfort and that can withstand enough force in relation to your puppy's size. Practice putting it on and off her in the house, using treats as rewards, so that both of you can get used to how it fits. Don't let her play with it or chew on it. If you find that your puppy wants to chew on her seatbelt, use a chew deterrent spray on it to discourage her.

You can find canine seat belts at your local or online pet store retailer. You'll also find other products to keep your puppy safely confined in the car. Always secure her in a backseat. If you have passenger-side airbags, they can kill your puppy if deployed.

It's important that you don't use the car only to take your puppy to the veterinarian's office. Hopefully, you've started training her to recognize the veterinarian's office as a wonderful place. It can still be scary for your puppy, though, so you don't want her to associate car rides with shots or other scary instances. This exercise will help your puppy learn that car rides are fun. It can be especially useful for puppies who get carsick.

STEP 1:

a) Have treats handy. Put your puppy in the car and secure her in her crate or seatbelt. Mark "Yes!" and give her a treat.

b) If your puppy is happy and enjoying this, go on to Step 2.

c) If she seems unsure or fearful, take her out of the car casually. Do not make a fuss over her. Put her back in the car and confine her in her crate or seatbelt. Mark "Yes," give her a treat, and praise her. Repeat a couple times, then take a break. Stay with this until she is more comfortable in the car.

STEP 2:

a) Take your puppy for a short drive around the block. If she is quiet and behaving, mark "Yes" and praise her.

b) If your puppy is happy and enjoying this, go on to Step 3.

c) If your puppy is unsure or seems fearful, take smaller steps. Instead of going all the way around the block, just go down your driveway. You may feel silly, but you'll be doing a great service to your puppy by helping her become used to car rides that she'll need for a lifetime. When she is more comfortable, go on to Step 3.

STEP 3:

a) Go for longer rides. Make sure that they are all positive experiences. For example, take her for a short ride to visit a friend and his dog so that your puppy can enjoy a safe play

The crate is an indispensable item to pack when traveling.

date.

b) If you find that your puppy gets carsick, take shorter rides and try to build up to longer ones. If she still gets carsick, talk with your veterinarian about possible medications that can help.

Traveling by Airplane

If you want to take your puppy on a plane, you need to make a lot of preparations beforehand. Don't wait until the last minute before making your plans. Airlines are experiencing many changes with security and company mergers, and what was acceptable a year ago may not be today. Also, be sure to check with your specific airline, because the rules may not be the same from one airline to another.

In general, if you have a puppy small enough to fit in an approved carrier that will fit under the seat of an airplane, she will be eligible to fly in the cabin. Airlines regulate how many dogs can fly in the cabin, so get your reservation early. There will be an extra charge. If your puppy is larger, she will have to fly in the cargo area in an approved carrier. Some airlines will not allow certain flat-faced breeds, such as Bulldogs or Pugs, to fly during warmer months because they can have breathing difficulties. Because your puppy will have to fly in a crate, it's important that you crate train her before her flight, or she could become stressed and traumatized.

You must get a health certificate from your veterinarian within

Your patient, well-behaved puppy may be a good candidate for therapy work.

a certain time before your flight. Talk with your veterinarian if you're thinking of using tranquilizers or sedatives—he may not recommend them because they can have adverse affects. Also, make sure that your puppy has proper ID. Follow all airline directions carefully about labeling the crate and providing food and water.

Write down the names of airline personnel who help you with your plans, and keep them with you. Keep in close contact with airline staff in case of any flight delays or cancellations, and talk with them ahead of time about what to do should you experience them during your flight. For example, if you have to change planes on your trip, and you've completed the first leg and have an unexpected four-hour delay before boarding your next plane, what will happen to your puppy? If possible, it's best to book direct flights.

During your trip, make sure that you see your puppy being put on the plane. If you have to change planes, make sure that you see your puppy being removed from the first plane and put on the next plane. Most airline personnel are happy to assist you. Should you run into one who wants to simply reassure you that everything is taken care of, you may have to get politely assertive. Don't be afraid to speak up for your puppy. Mistakes *do* happen, and you don't want your puppy to end up in one place and you somewhere else.

Volunteering: Animal-Assisted Activities and Therapy

Sharing your dog with patients in health care facilities can be wonderfully rewarding. Animal-assisted activities are friendly visits with patients by a therapy team. Taking a therapy dog to a nursing home to cheer the residents is an example of an animal-assisted activity. Animal-assisted therapy is treatment prescribed by a health care professional for a patient involving a therapy team. For example, a physical therapist may request that a therapy team assist a patient who has had a stroke. If the patient brushes the therapy dog or throws a ball for her to fetch, he is exercising his muscles and hand–eye coordination.

Puppies who make good therapy dogs are social, friendly, confident, and love to be handled all over their bodies, even by strangers. They must have excellent obedience skills because they may be working with some very fragile people, so they must be under control at all times. They must be well behaved in different environments, and they cannot be skittish or fearful.

You can start training your puppy for therapy work at a very young age, but she will not be eligible for a national program until she is one year old. Getting registered with a national program is important, because the program will provide you with the education and training that you need to have safe, effective visits. You'll be evaluated to make sure that you and your puppy have the right skills and aptitude for this kind of volunteer work. You'll also benefit from liability insurance, so you'll be protected in case you have an incident.

If you'd like to volunteer with your puppy in animal-assisted activities and therapy, contact one of the national programs that register teams and learn about their requirements. If you have a local group that volunteers with their pets, contact them for tips on how to get involved. Start training your puppy in good family manners, and make sure that she receives plenty of positive socialization. She already brings you great joy —maybe she will grow up to be a dog who is able to share that joy with others!

Roger Caras, an Emmy award-winning broadcaster and former host of the Westminster Kennel Club dog show, once said, "Dogs are not our whole life, but they make our lives whole." Your puppy will grow up to be a lifelong friend and partner in life. Share your life with her by finding things that you can do together. Both of your lives will be that much richer for the time you share.

Chapter 8

HEALTH
of Your Puppy

With all the diseases, parasites, and injuries that can befall your puppy, you may be tempted to wrap her up in a plastic bubble to keep her safe. That may not be practical—but you can learn how to protect your puppy by providing her with quality health care.

THE VETERINARIAN

When you add a puppy to your family, you also need to make an important addition to your address book and cell phone speed dial: her doctor. Your puppy's veterinarian will provide important preventive and medical care.

Choosing a Veterinarian

One of the most important things that you can do for your puppy is to find her a quality veterinarian, preferably for her lifetime. Choose a veterinarian before you even take your puppy home. Ideally, you should bring your puppy for an initial checkup within 48 hours of bringing her home. Some breeders or rescue groups may even specify that in their contracts.

Find References

Ask your friends, family, and coworkers if they are happy with their choice in veterinarian. If you belong to a dog sport club, ask for referrals from your fellow members.

What other people may find appealing in a veterinarian may not hold the same appeal for you, but asking them is a great place to start your research. You also can look in your telephone and online directories, or contact your state's veterinary medical association and ask for a list of veterinarians in your area.

You can train your puppy to enjoy veterinary visits.

Make an Interview Appointment

What sounds great on paper or through a friend's description may be completely different in person. So call the practice you are considering and make an appointment to meet the veterinarian and support staff and to check out the practice to see if it's the one you want for your puppy. You want to make an appointment so that you can be sure to meet the veterinarian. If you just show up, you may be able to talk with the support staff, but the veterinarian likely will be busy with patients.

Some veterinarians may charge you for an appointment, even if you're coming by yourself. Don't let that scare you off. You are asking for a block of time, just like a regular patient. You will also be asking for information and expecting the veterinarian to answer your questions, so he is still offering you a service. Some veterinarians won't charge you or may charge a reduced fee. When you call for the appointment, be sure to explain that you are interviewing practices because you are getting a puppy, and ask them about any related fees.

What to Look for in a Quality Veterinary Practice

Facility: Is it clean? Is it free of unpleasant odors? Are the grounds outside well kept? If there are boarding or grooming services also available that you would use, are they clean and free of unpleasant odors? Is the practice in a good location and easy to get in and out of?

Experience: How long has the veterinarian been in practice? If you have a breed with special concerns, how familiar is he with caring for them? If you are training your dog for sports activities, how familiar is he with treating canine athletes?

Office Hours: What are the office hours? When are the doctors available for appointments? Are these hours compatible with your availability?

Appointments: How long does it take the practice to answer the phone? How long is someone kept on hold? Is the staff friendly and helpful over the phone? How long does it take to get an appointment for a well-puppy visit versus a sick puppy visit? If there are several doctors in the practice, can you pick a specific doctor? Who covers the practice if a doctor is sick or on vacation?

Emergencies: How does the practice handle emergencies during regular office hours? Do they offer work-in appointments? How does the practice handle emergencies after office hours or on holidays?

Services: What services are available? Does the practice provide medical exams? Surgeries (and if so, what kind)? X-rays? Dentistry? Nutrition counseling? Laboratory testing? What about other services, such as boarding and grooming? Is the veterinarian willing to refer to a specialist if necessary? If so, who are the specialists they recommend?

Fees and Payment: What methods of payment are accepted? Does the practice require immediate payment for services, or does it bill? Are payment plans available? What is the typical fee for a well-puppy visit, annual exam, dentistry, and neutering surgery?

Staff: Are the doctors in the practice members of professional associations? Do they all pursue continuing education to keep up with the latest information? Are you comfortable with the veterinarian? Is the doctor knowledgeable, friendly, and willing to answer your questions? What about the support staff? You will probably interact with the support staff more than with the doctor, so you want to be comfortable with the entire practice package. Is the support staff friendly, courteous, knowledgeable, and willing to answer your questions? Does the staff treat clients and their clients' pets with respect? Are they patient with frightened or nervous animals? If you begin to wish that you could come to this practice for your own health care, then you've probably found a caring, professional place to take your puppy.

Bring a Sample

Take a fresh stool sample with you to your puppy's veterinary appointment. They'll need to check your puppy's feces for parasites. If you don't bring a sample, then they'll need to insert an instrument into your puppy's rectum to get one. That could be unpleasant and frightening for your puppy (and squeamish for you). Make it easier on everyone and bring a sample for testing.

Puppy's First Visit

One of the first things that you should do after bringing your puppy home is to take her to your veterinarian for a thorough checkup. If there is anything wrong, you want to know about it right away. It's a daunting thought, but it may even affect whether or not you keep your puppy. Should your veterinarian find a serious or genetic problem, you will have to make a decision about whether or not you will be able to face the associated risks, problems, and medical costs of keeping the puppy.

During your puppy's first visit, a veterinary technician will take her temperature and weight. Depending on your puppy's age and previous care, the vet also may take blood to test for heartworms. Your veterinarian should give your puppy a thorough examination. The doctor will be checking for general health issues, genetic problems, and parasites. The doctor may administer vaccines, depending on how many your puppy has already had.

Be sure to discuss any concerns you may have with your veterinarian. If something feels wrong to you, or if you're unsure of something, let the doctor know.

Teaching Your Puppy to Love Veterinary Visits

Even if you have chosen the most caring veterinarian and office support staff in the world, the doctor's office can be a scary place for a puppy. Your puppy can hear and smell things you can't, things that could be frightening to her. The staff will insert a thermometer into her rectum and give her injections, which could be startling or unpleasant.

Puppies who are afraid will whine, tremble, bark, or even act aggressively. If your veterinarian goes to examine your puppy and she growls, it's probably because she is frightened. Your puppy will have to visit the veterinarian all her life, so it's important that she be as comfortable as possible when she's there. You don't have to leave that to chance—you can train your puppy to enjoy her veterinary office visits.

The vet will examine your puppy from head to tail.

Give Her a Comfort Rug
STEP 1:

Purchase a small bath rug that's machine washable, with a rubber backing to prevent slipping. When you feed your puppy her regularly scheduled meals, put the bowl on this rug.

Throughout the day, toss some treats onto the rug so that your puppy starts to associate the rug with good things. Don't let her chew on the rug.

Throughout the day, bring your puppy to the rug and place her on it, petting her and giving her affection.

STEP 2:

When it's time to take your puppy to the vet's office, take her comfort rug. Place it on the examination table. Those tables are very slippery, and this will give her some traction so that she will feel more secure.

When you get home, toss the rug in the washing machine. When it's dry, put it back in place for your puppy's next meal.

Play Doctor

This exercise will help to teach your puppy to enjoy being examined, which will make it much easier for you and your veterinarian to care for her.

STEP 1:

a) Have some treats handy. Put your puppy's comfort rug on a table or counter. Put your puppy on the rug, and give her a treat.

STEP 2:

Now you are going to examine your puppy. You'll do it in short steps, rewarding your puppy for each action that goes well. Only reward your puppy if she lets you examine her. If she's overly wiggly or starts to mouth you, don't mark the behavior and don't give her a treat. Instead, take it slower and work more gradually.

a) Hold her head and look in her eyes briefly. Mark the behavior with the word "Yes!" and give her a treat.

b) Look in one ear. Mark with a "Yes!" and give her a treat. Look in the other ear. Mark with a "Yes!" and give her a treat.

c) Look at her teeth. Mark with a "Yes!" and give her a treat.

d) Examine each paw. Mark with a "Yes!" and give her a treat for each paw.

e) Examine her rear end and tail. Mark with a "Yes!" and give her a treat.

f) Put one hand under her belly. Lift her slightly off the table or counter. Mark with a "Yes!" and give her a treat.

g) Put one hand under her belly and squeeze slightly. Mark with a "Yes!" and give her a treat.

h) Practice your examination at least once a day, and vary your routine each time. For example, you may start by examining her head first one time, and then the next time, start with her paws.

Troubleshooting

What if your puppy simply refuses to let you do something, like check her teeth? You don't want to scare her by grabbing her mouth, but she does need to learn that you must be able to examine all parts of her body. To teach her this, first get some really good treats. Start by just briefly touching her sensitive areas, then marking with a "Yes!" and giving her the treat. Do this over several sessions. Gradually, work up to being able to examine the area.

Veterinary Office Etiquette

It's never polite or safe to let your puppy run up to another animal, let alone in a veterinarian's office. What if that animal is sick and has a contagious disease? Or what if that animal is frightened? He could lash out at your puppy and cause her harm. Always keep your puppy on leash (even if you carry her in, just in case), and keep her close to you in the office.

You may find that some people forget their manners in a veterinarian's office, too. Some will flock to your cute puppy and want to pet her without asking. If your puppy is healthy, and you're okay with the interaction, then use the attention for socialization.

But if your puppy is not feeling well, don't let people pet her. Just explain that she is sick and you think it's best for her to be left alone until she's feeling better.

STEP 3:

Once your puppy allows you and your family to examine her all over, ask your friends to take on the role of veterinarian and examine her, too.

a) While your friend performs the examination, mark each portion with a "Yes!" and give your puppy the treats.

STEP 4:

a) When your puppy is enjoying her examinations and is behaving herself without being too wiggly or mouthy, it's time to wean her off so many treats. Start combining parts of the exam. For example, look at her ears and teeth, then mark with a "Yes!" and give her a treat.

Remember, a veterinary office is not the same as your living room. Your puppy may do great at home but still get nervous or fidgety at the vet's office. So, when you take your puppy to the veterinarian's office, bring your treats with you and reward her occasionally throughout her exam.

Training Visits

One of the best ways to prevent fear and aggression at the vet's office is to take your puppy to the office just to socialize. This way, she will learn that not all visits mean shots.

Bring some treats, and ask the staff to give them to your puppy. If there are people waiting in the lobby who don't have their hands full with their own pets, ask them to give your puppy treats, too.

When you first get your puppy, it will seem as though you are at the veterinarian's office all the time, and taking her to the office for extra visits may seem like an added inconvenience. This pace won't last, though. Once your puppy gets her last round of shots, hopefully she won't need to go to the vet unless it's time for her annual visits. By making socialization visits now, you'll help to ensure that those later visits go much more smoothly.

Annual Examinations

Plan on taking your puppy to see the veterinarian at least once each year for an annual checkup. These visits are very important, because problems that go undiagnosed could be life threatening. Also, some dogs are very stoic, so they could be in pain but you'd never know it. A comprehensive physical exam can help your veterinarian discover potential problems.

During the annual visit, the staff will weigh your puppy, take her temperature, and check her heart rate and respiration. They'll inspect a stool sample for parasites. They'll also take blood from your puppy to check for heartworms. Even if you have diligently given your puppy her heartworm prevention medication each month, this laboratory test is still necessary to make sure that no heartworms are present.

Adequate exercise will result in a happier, healthier puppy.

The veterinarian will examine her from head to tail. This includes checking her ears for signs of infection or parasites. He will check her eyes for cataracts and retinal disease. Your puppy's mouth will be examined for abscesses or tumors. Her teeth will be checked for cracks and tartar buildup and to see if any are missing. The veterinarian also will check her gums and listen to her heart and lungs. He will feel her abdomen to make sure that all the organs are the right size and that no abnormalities are present. In addition, he will inspect her skin for parasites, "hot spots," or other problems. Your puppy will then receive any vaccinations that she may need.

The annual exam is a good opportunity for you to touch base with your veterinarian about your puppy's growth and progress and to share any concerns or questions that you may have. Don't be afraid to ask questions. Your puppy depends on you for her health care, so make the most of your veterinarian's expertise.

NEUTERING YOUR PUPPY

Neutering involves the removal of the entire uterus, ovaries, and fallopian tubes (also called "spaying") for female dogs, and the removal of both testicles (also known as "castration") for male dogs. Both spaying and castrating are major surgeries, but they are also the most common surgeries that veterinarians perform.

Neutering Myths and Facts

Neutering a puppy can be a sensitive topic for some people. With some couples, one supports the surgery while the other doesn't even want to talk about it. It's important to decide what's best for your puppy and for your family when considering neutering. Get the facts.

Myth: Neutering will change my puppy's personality.

Fact: Your puppy's personality is made up of a lot more than reproductive organs. Puppies are still masculine or feminine after the surgery, and it doesn't affect their ability to play or participate in dog activities or sports. There is an added benefit to neutering males: The reduction of testosterone reduces the biological need for them to search for a female in heat, which makes males less likely to roam.

Myth: Neutering will make my puppy fat.

Fact: People make dogs fat. If you overfeed your puppy and don't give her the proper amount of exercise, she will gain weight.

Myth: A female dog should have at least one litter to feel fulfilled.

Fact: Your female does not stay up at night worrying about her biological clock. Getting pregnant, even one time, will not improve her behavior. The mating instinct actually can lead to undesirable behaviors and stress for you and your pet.

Why Neuter?

The truth is, there are certain benefits to neutering both male and female puppies.

Females

Female dogs usually come into heat between six months and one year of age. Small-breed dogs tend to come into heat earlier than do large-breed dogs. Females then have a heat cycle about every six months, depending on the breed, which can last as long as 21 days. During this time, a female will start to bleed and may become anxious and irritable. *As long as your female is in heat, you cannot leave her unsupervised for even a second!* Don't think that a fence will stop an intact male dog from getting to your girl. They will dig under, climb over, and do anything to respond to their hormonal instincts.

If you spay your female, you'll eliminate the heat cycle and the

Should You Breed?

If you're thinking about breeding your puppy, please be sure that you are making the right decision for your pet and your family. You may think that you'll easily be able to find homes for all the offspring, but shelters are full of puppies, including purebreds, whose breeders thought the same thing.

Ask your veterinarian about the risks involved with breeding. Talk to reputable breeders about the pros and cons. Also, contact your breed's national or local rescue organization for a wonderful resource on why your puppy's breed often ends up abandoned. If you are going to bring more puppies into this world, make sure that you're doing it for the right reasons.

stress that comes along with it. You also will reduce her risk of certain health problems, such as uterine infections and mammary cancer.

Males

Male dogs are capable of breeding at as young as six months of age. They tend to "mark" their territory by spraying strong-smelling urine on your house, furniture, and other belongings. Males also will follow their natural hormonal instincts to find a female dog in heat. This isn't a longing for a nice girl to settle down with and build a family—it's a strong hormonal urge. Male dogs will run right into the road following that scent. They will fight other dogs over a female and can get seriously hurt or even killed.

Contrary to popular myth, neutering will not change your puppy's personality.

If you neuter your male, he will focus more on you instead of his hormones. He will also have a lower risk of contracting certain health problems, such as prostate disease, testicular cancer, and infections.

The Best Time to Neuter

When should you neuter your puppy? The American Veterinary Medical Association (AVMA), the Humane Society of the United States (HSUS), and other organizations all agree that it is safe to neuter puppies as early as eight weeks of age. Many shelters and rescue organizations are neutering very young puppies before they place them in their homes to help to reduce the pet overpopulation. Talk to your veterinarian about the best time to neuter your puppy.

VACCINATIONS

Vaccinations can help to protect your puppy against certain diseases. They are health products that trigger your puppy's immune system to kick in and fight future infections.

How Vaccines Work

Very young puppies are vulnerable to infectious diseases. Your puppy absorbed antibodies from her mother's milk, mostly during her first 24 hours of life. If your puppy's mother had a recent set of shots, she had a lot of antibodies to pass on to her puppies. If your puppy's mother was not up to date on her vaccinations, then she had fewer antibodies to pass on to her puppies.

Antibodies protect your puppy from certain illnesses. They also prevent vaccines from taking hold very well. These antibodies don't last, however—they start disappearing between 6 and 16 weeks of age. As the antibodies disappear, your puppy becomes more vulnerable to diseases. This is why veterinarians usually administer shots so often during a puppy's first 12 to 16 weeks; they want the vaccines to take hold as soon as the mother's antibodies are gone.

The Vaccine Debate

In the past, puppies commonly were given a set of vaccinations, then received boosters each year thereafter. As more is learned about diseases and canine immune systems, it has become evident that the immunity that some vaccines trigger can protect dogs for longer than one year. Current research also shows that some vaccines may not last an entire year. Some people have concerns that their dogs are getting too many vaccines, and wonder if they could be causing illnesses. Your puppy's breeder may even have told you not to get all the shots at once or to delay the rabies shot until your puppy was older.

Just as with any medical procedure, vaccines present risks. While most dogs respond well to vaccines, some do not develop the desired immunity response. Although this is rare, these dogs can possibly become ill. Other dogs can have adverse reactions. The most common are usually mild and short term, including fever, reduced appetite, sluggishness, and pain or swelling at the site of the vaccination. Rarely, some dogs can develop more serious reactions. If your puppy experiences repeated vomiting or diarrhea, whole body itching, difficulty breathing, collapse, or swelling of the face and legs, call your veterinarian or veterinary emergency clinic immediately. She may be having a serious allergic reaction.

Now that you know the risks of vaccination, is it still a good idea to get your puppy vaccinated? Absolutely. Your puppy is extremely vulnerable to deadly diseases. Vaccines can help to

prevent her from becoming infected. Vaccinations have helped to prevent deaths in millions of animals over the years. Just as human children still get shots to help protect them, your puppy needs protection through vaccination, too.

Talk to your veterinarian about any concerns that you have about vaccinations. Today, the American Veterinary Medical Association (AVMA) recommends that veterinarians offer a "core" set of vaccinations and present the option of "noncore" vaccines for dogs with special needs. Just because a wide variety of vaccines is available doesn't mean that your puppy needs all of them. For example, your dog may live in a part of the country that has a higher incidence of a particular disease. Or perhaps you plan to compete in dog sports with your puppy, which could expose her to other specific diseases. As your puppy grows, she also may have different vaccination requirements. Work with your veterinarian to customize a vaccination schedule for your puppy.

Diseases and Their Vaccines

It may seem like your puppy is a pincushion during her first few months. What exactly do the shots protect her from? What do all those initials mean on the veterinary office receipt? Here's the scoop on common diseases and their vaccines.

Canine Coronavirus

Canine coronavirus is a disease caused by a virus that attacks the intestines. It's usually mild but can be severe in young puppies or dogs with weak immune systems. Your puppy can catch this disease by being exposed to the feces of infected dogs.

Symptoms include depression, loss of appetite, vomiting, and a foul-smelling yellow to orange diarrhea. The diarrhea may be bloody.

Treatment includes giving fluids and controlling vomiting and diarrhea. A vaccine is available for coronavirus, which is sometimes considered optional.

Canine Distemper

Canine distemper is a very contagious and serious disease caused by a virus that attacks the respiratory, gastrointestinal, and sometimes the nervous systems of puppies and dogs. It also can infect some wild animals, including skunks, foxes, coyotes,

Vaccinations can help to prevent your puppy against certain diseases.

wolves, raccoons, and ferrets. Your puppy can catch canine distemper by inhaling the virus, which is shed in the respiratory secretions of infected animals.

All dogs are at risk for canine distemper. Puppies less than four months of age who have not had the canine distemper vaccine are especially at risk.

Symptoms include a watery, pus-like eye discharge, nasal discharge, fever, coughing, reduced appetite, lethargy, vomiting, and diarrhea. As the disease progresses, it can cause seizures or paralysis. Sometimes, it causes footpads to harden. The disease is usually fatal. If a dog doesn't die from distemper, the virus can cause permanent damage to her nervous system.

No medication is available to kill distemper in infected dogs. In lieu of drugs, treatment includes fluids, prevention of secondary infections, and controlling vomiting, diarrhea, and neurological symptoms. Puppies should receive a series of vaccinations during their first months to help to prevent this deadly disease.

Canine Infectious Tracheobronchitis (Kennel Cough)

Canine infectious tracheobronchitis, or kennel cough, is a group of highly contagious respiratory diseases. The name "kennel cough" originated because the disease spreads quickly, especially among dogs in boarding kennels. Several viruses and bacteria can cause kennel cough, and a dog can have one or a few of them and contract the disease. Your puppy can become infected by inhaling the respiratory secretions of infected dogs.

Symptoms include a harsh, dry, hacking cough and sometimes gagging or retching. Most dogs still have a good appetite and appear healthy, other than the cough, with no fever. Puppies and toy breeds can be especially vulnerable, however, to nasal congestion, which can cause complications. Some dogs with severe cases of kennel cough can develop pneumonia. Symptoms include depression, a low-grade fever, loss of appetite, moist cough, nasal discharge, wheezing, and rapid breathing.

Treatment depends on the severity of the disease. Your veterinarian may prescribe antibiotics. Severe cases may require hospitalization. Some vaccines can help to prevent kennel cough, although because it can be caused by one or more microorganisms, it is difficult to prevent completely.

Canine Parvovirus

Canine parvovirus is a highly contagious, serious disease caused by a virus that attacks the gastrointestinal system. It also can damage the heart muscle in very young and unborn puppies. Your puppy can contract this disease by ingesting the virus, which exists in the stool of an infected dog. For example, if your puppy walks through your neighborhood, steps in the feces of an infected dog, and then later licks her paws, she could become infected with the disease. If you walk where an infected dog has been, you could even track the virus home on your shoes. Parvovirus can survive for long periods of time and doesn't die easily, even with environmental changes.

All dogs are at risk for parvovirus. Puppies less than four months of age who have not had the canine parvovirus vaccine are especially at risk. Certain breeds, including Rottweilers and Dobermans, also seem to have a higher risk for the disease.

Kennel cough spreads quickly, especially among dogs in boarding kennels.

Symptoms include lethargy, loss of appetite, fever, vomiting, and severe, usually bloody diarrhea. Dehydration sets in quickly, and most deaths occur within 72 hours once symptoms appear.

No drug can kill the virus in infected dogs. Treatment includes fluids, controlling vomiting and diarrhea, and preventing secondary infections. Puppies should receive a series of vaccinations during their first months to help to prevent this deadly disease.

Infectious Hepatitis

Infectious hepatitis is a highly contagious disease caused by a virus that attacks the liver, kidneys, and lining of the blood vessels. Most cases occur in puppies less than one year of age. It is more common in unvaccinated dogs and wild canines, such as foxes and coyotes. (This type of hepatitis does not cause hepatitis in people.) Your puppy can catch the disease by coming into contact with an infected dog's stools, saliva, or urine.

Symptoms depend on the severity of the infection and can include loss of appetite, lethargy, bloody diarrhea, high fever, vomiting, and collapse. Dogs may tuck up their bellies, indicating pain in the liver. Light may be painful to their eyes, causing tearing and squinting.

Treatment of infectious hepatitis varies depending on the severity of the illness. Severe cases require hospitalization. A vaccine is available to help to prevent this disease. It is usually incorporated into the DHPP (distemper, hepatitis, parainfluenza, parvovirus) shot. Your veterinarian may recommend a series of shots until your puppy is about 16 weeks old, and then encourage booster shots as necessary.

For Prevention, Pick Up Your Pup!

Canine parvovirus is a very contagious, persistent virus. Canine distemper also can be deadly. In addition to getting your puppy vaccinated against these diseases, you can do other things to avoid infection. Don't let your puppy walk where unknown dogs have been, and don't let her gather with unknown puppies or dogs. This includes at pet supply stores, around your neighborhood, and in other public areas. If an infected dog has been in those places, your puppy could easily pick up the virus. If you must take her to those places, carry her. Also, carry her into the veterinarian's office, and keep her in a crate or in your arms until she has been fully vaccinated.

Leptospirosis

Leptospirosis is a disease caused by bacteria that mainly attack the kidneys and liver. Your puppy can catch leptospirosis by coming into contact with urine from infected animals. Other animals who carry this disease include cows, rats, pigs, skunks, and opossums. If your puppy drinks water contaminated by infected urine, or if it enters a break in her skin, she could become infected. Dogs who spend a lot of time in the water have a higher risk of contracting leptospirosis. (The bacterium also causes a disease in people called "Weil's disease." People contract it in the same way that dogs do.)

Symptoms include fever, depression, loss of appetite, vomiting, lethargy, and muscle pain. Diarrhea or bloody urine may be present. In severe cases, the whites of the eye turn yellow from jaundice, and blood may appear in the stool.

Treatment includes fluids, antibiotics, controlling vomiting and diarrhea, and sometimes hospitalization. A vaccine exists that helps to protect against leptospirosis. It is usually included in the DHLPP (distemper, hepatitis, leptospirosis, parainfluenza, parvovirus) combination vaccine, which can be given several times before a puppy reaches four months of age, and then given as a booster shot annually afterward. Most veterinarians currently consider the

Lyme disease is more common in wooded areas.

leptospirosis vaccine to be optional because it often causes allergic reactions.

Lyme Disease

Lyme disease is caused by a bacteria that mainly attacks the joints. Ticks become infected when they ingest blood from infected mice and birds. Your puppy can then get Lyme disease when an infected tick bites her. Dogs can't spread Lyme disease to humans if they are infected, but they *can* spread the ticks carrying the disease.

Lyme disease is considered the most common tick-borne illness in the United States. It's spread during tick season, mainly May through August. It is most common in wooded areas of the Northeast, upper Midwest, northern California, and the Pacific Northwest.

Symptoms include sudden lameness and painful or swollen joints. Some dogs may run a fever, feel weak and lethargic, and lose weight.

Treatment of Lyme disease includes the administration of antibiotics. An optional vaccine is available to help to prevent the disease.

Rabies

Rabies is a deadly disease caused by a virus that attacks the nervous system. Most cases of rabies occur in wild animals, especially skunks, raccoons, bats, and foxes. Your puppy can contract rabies when bitten by an infected animal. (So can you!)

Symptoms include personality changes, chewing at the site where the virus entered the body, withdrawal, staring into space, viciousness, aggressiveness, fearlessness, drooling, gagging, foaming at the mouth, and paralysis.

There is no cure for rabies; the disease is fatal. Fortunately, the rabies vaccine has proven effective in preventing rabies in most pets. Your puppy usually will receive her first rabies shot at about three months of age. Consult your veterinarian about booster shots, which can be given as one-year or three-year vaccinations. Your individual state also may have requirements about how often your puppy should receive a rabies vaccine.

PARASITES

Worms. Ticks. Fleas. Mites. Sounds like a bad horror movie! But if you have a puppy, you're likely to encounter these nasty critters as part of the package. They may give you the creepy crawlies, but you must learn how to protect your puppy against them to help prevent diseases and other health problems.

External Parasites

External parasites are those that latch onto the outside of your puppy to do their damage.

Demodectic Mange Mites

When people hear a veterinary diagnosis of "mange," they often become alarmed because they believe that their puppy is contagious. But there are different types of mange, and demodectic mange is not the contagious kind.

Demodectic mange is caused by a type of mite, which is a tiny insect. Most puppies get these mites from their mothers during the first days of their lives, which is normal. If a puppy's immune system isn't working properly, however, the mites multiply out of control, causing disease. It most frequently occurs in puppies and in adult dogs with poor immune systems. Some studies have shown a genetic tendency.

Two different types of demodectic mange occur: localized and generalized. Localized demodectic mange occurs in puppies less than one year old. Symptoms include a thinning of the fur around the eyes, lips, and corners of the mouth. Sometimes hair loss on the legs and feet occurs. The thinning becomes worse until patches about 1 inch (2.5 cm) in diameter are missing. The skin can become scaly, red, and infected. Localized demodectic mange usually heals by itself in a couple of months, but it can come and go. Treatment includes a topical ointment rubbed into the thinning patches. If more than five patches exist, the disease may be developing into generalized demodectic mange.

Although generalized demodectic mange can be a progression of the localized variety, sometimes it spontaneously occurs in adult dogs. Generalized demodectic mange involves large, thinning patches on the head, legs, and body. The mites cause the skin to break down and form crusty sores. This can be extremely uncomfortable and painful for a dog, and the condition requires veterinary assistance. Treatment includes medicated dips and shampoos and often antibiotics for skin infections.

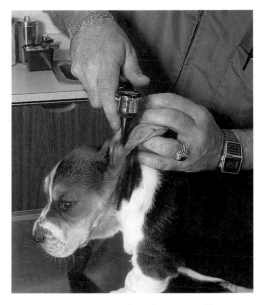

Consult your vet if you suspect that your puppy has ear mites.

Ear Mites

One of the most common causes of ear symptoms in puppies and young adult dogs is a tiny insect called an ear mite. Ear mites live in the ear canals and feed by piercing a puppy's skin. They are very contagious to dogs (and cats) but not to people.

If your puppy has ear mites, she will scratch her ears vigorously and violently shake her head. That's because ear mites cause a severe hypersensitive reaction and intense itching. Your puppy's earflaps will become red, crusted, and scabbed. Her ear canal will have a dry, crumbly, dark brown, waxy discharge. Her ears may have a bad odor due to a secondary infection. If both of your puppy's ears are involved, ear mites are a likely cause of the problem.

Consult your veterinarian if you suspect that your puppy has ear mites. You must apply medication in her ears, and you'll have to diligently clean them so that the medication can reach the canal thoroughly. Your veterinarian may recommend that you treat all dogs and cats in your home, because ear mites are so contagious. During treatment, the mites may flee the ears and take up residence on another part of your puppy's body, causing her to itch. Talk to your veterinarian about using a topical treatment on your puppy to help to ease her discomfort and kill any mites that try to escape.

Fleas

Fleas are small, dark brown to black insects that feed on blood. These persistent little parasites prefer warm, humid environments. They have powerful back legs and can jump considerable distances. Fleas move through your dog's fur very rapidly and can be very hard to catch.

In most dogs, flea bites cause mild itching. In young puppies or with severe infestations, they can cause anemia and even death. Some dogs develop allergies to flea saliva and can experience severe itching, loss of fur, and skin infections.

If your puppy is scratching, run a fine-toothed comb through her fur. Be sure to check her belly, around her tail and groin area, and her back. If you see little dark specks of what look like dirt, they are probably flea feces. These are actually bits of digested blood. If you were to smear them on a wet paper towel, they would be a reddish brown color. You also may see tiny white specks, which are flea eggs.

Controlling fleas is a multi-step process because of their life cycle. During her lifetime, a female flea can lay hundreds of eggs. These eggs fall off your puppy and incubate in carpets, beneath furniture, and in cracks and bedding. They hatch in one to ten days as slender, whitish worm-like larvae. The larvae avoid light and burrow into carpet or outside dirt. They feed on small bits of animal or plant debris and adult flea feces until they are fully grown, which can be from five days

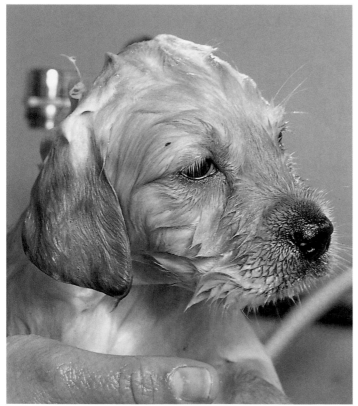

A flea shampoo is one option for killing these external parasites.

to three weeks. The larvae then spin cocoons, where they develop into a pupa and then an adult. The cocoon protects the larvae from insecticides. Fleas can stay in their cocoons from less than a week to more than four months. Adult fleas come out of their cocoons after a physical disturbance or when they sense warm-blooded animals. After hatching, adult fleas have about two weeks to find a host before they die.

Because your house could have flea eggs, larvae, protected larvae in cocoons, and adult fleas at any given time, it's important to use a multi-step flea control program. Often, one form of control will not kill all life stages of the flea. Do your research first, however, so that you don't put too many poisons in your puppy's environment. The combination that you choose must be safe for your puppy and your family.

Talk with your veterinarian about the different types of flea treatments available for your puppy. Some are not appropriate for very young or small puppies, so it's important to find out what's safe. Here are some of the most common:

- *Pills:* Some treatments come in the form of a pill. When a flea bites your puppy, it ingests the medication, which helps to prevent flea eggs from fully maturing. This type of treatment doesn't kill adult fleas, however, so it will take time to reduce the entire flea population in your home if you have a bad infestation. You usually use this type of treatment along with a topical treatment to kill adult fleas. It also requires the flea to bite your puppy, so if your puppy develops an allergy to flea bites, this method may not be your best option. Some pills combine heartworm preventive with flea treatment.

- *Liquids:* Other treatments include liquids that you apply between your puppy's shoulder blades. These kill adult fleas before they've had a chance to reproduce. The flea does not have to bite your puppy for the treatment to work, because it kills fleas on contact. A single treatment can last for 30 or more days and can remain effective even if your puppy gets wet, depending on the brand. Some liquids also kill ticks, and others contain heartworm preventive.

- *Flea Shampoos:* Flea shampoos will kill fleas only when they are on your puppy. Once you rinse them off, they have no residual effect.

- *Powders and Dusts:* Flea powders and dusts last longer than

shampoos, but you have to work them down through your puppy's coat onto her skin thoroughly. They can make your puppy's coat dry and gritty.

- *Sprays, Dips, and Foams:* Flea sprays, dips, and foams may be good choices if you have a bad infestation, or if your puppy is allergic to flea bites. Depending on the brand, they can kill fleas for up to a couple of weeks. A water-based spray may be preferable to an alcohol-based spray because it is less likely to dry out your puppy's coat, and it won't be flammable. If you use spray or foam on your puppy, start behind her neck and move downward, toward her tail. This will prevent the fleas from fleeing toward her face and ears. Flea dips soak all the way to the skin, where they quickly kill the parasites and have a long-lasting effect. Sprays, dips, and foams are among the most toxic flea treatments, so always consult your veterinarian before using them.
- *Collars:* Flea collars can help but won't kill all fleas. They don't cover your dog the way other treatments can and must be replaced frequently. Never let your puppy chew or bite a flea collar.

Before you apply any pesticides, wash your puppy's bedding. Thoroughly vacuum your home with a heavy-duty or commercial vacuum cleaner. Vacuum carpets, floors, and all upholstery. If possible, have your carpets professionally cleaned. The beating brushes in a quality vacuum can remove one quarter of the flea larvae and over half of the flea eggs. Vacuuming is also a physical disturbance, so it stimulates fleas to leave their cocoons. After cleaning, take the vacuum outside, remove the bag, and discard it.

Once you've vacuumed, apply an insecticide to your home. Flea bombs are easy to use, but they are not very effective. They release chemicals all over a room, not just where fleas are located. Instead, use spot treatments with sprays directed at the floor. Treat wherever your puppy has access: carpets, under furniture near pet areas, and in floor edges and cracks. You don't have to treat the entire carpet or all floor areas. If your puppy is allowed on the furniture, treat under the cushions. Always check the product label for instructions and safety concerns.

Don't forget to treat your yard, too, or you'll miss an important step in your flea-killing program. Mow the grass first, and collect and discard the clippings. Treat the areas where your puppy has access.

You may have to repeat these steps several times to kill all the fleas as they emerge from their protective cocoons. You also may want to call a professional exterminator. He can help you get the problem under control so that you can focus on handling preventive maintenance afterward.

Ringworm

Ringworm is caused by a fungus that invades the hair and its follicles. It usually occurs in puppies and young adult dogs and commonly affects the ears, face, paws, and tail. Your puppy can get ringworm by coming into contact with ringworm spores in soil or the infected hair of dogs, cats, or people. People can get ringworm from dogs, and vice versa. Children especially are susceptible to ringworm infection.

Symptoms include a spreading circle of hair loss with scaly skin in the middle and a red ring around the edge. It can trigger a secondary infection with crusty, scabby skin that causes your puppy to scratch or lick. The symptoms of ringworm look like the symptoms of other diseases, so it's important to take your puppy to the veterinarian for an accurate diagnosis.

Treatment includes medication from your veterinarian. You must thoroughly clean your dog's toys and grooming supplies as well, and it may be a good idea to throw out her bedding. Thoroughly clean your home and clothing to prevent the spread of ringworm to the rest of your family. As long as your puppy has ringworm, don't let children touch her. If you have concerns about your family's health, consult your physician.

Sarcoptic Mange Mites

Sarcoptic mange, also known as scabies, is highly contagious. A tiny mite causes it. Your puppy can become infected with these mites by coming into direct contact with other animals who are infected or through contaminated grooming equipment or kennels.

Female mites burrow under a dog's skin to lay their eggs, which makes a dog feel itchy. Symptoms include severe scratching, hair loss, and swollen skin, usually around the ears, hocks, elbows, under the chest, and under the muzzle. In addition, the ear tips become crusty. As the disease progresses, it causes the skin to become thick, scaly, crusty, and dark.

Poisons to Other Pets

Some flea treatments may be safe for puppies but not for your cat or bird. If you have multiple animals, discuss a flea treatment program with your veterinarian before trying anything. You want to kill the fleas and keep your pets and family safe.

If your puppy has sarcoptic mange, your veterinarian will prescribe a treatment regimen, which can include medicated shampoos and dips, oral medication to kill the mites, steroids to relieve itching, and antibiotics for skin infections.

Ticks

Ticks are not insects; they are arachnids, related to spiders and mites. Their only source of food is blood. Most ticks are mainly found outdoors in grassy, weedy, or wooded areas. If your puppy comes into contact with them, they will cling to her and ride along. You also can bring them in on your clothing.

Ticks are dangerous because they can transmit several diseases to dogs and people, including Lyme disease. With severe infestations, dogs can lose a lot of blood and become anemic. Most ticks take several hours to transmit diseases, so if your puppy is exposed to an area that is likely to harbor ticks, it's important to inspect her frequently. Talk with your veterinarian about using a tick prevention medication, too.

You'll most likely find ticks latched onto your puppy's neck, in her ears, between her toes, or in the folds between her legs and body. Once a tick starts feeding on a dog, it is not likely to leave and latch onto a person.

If you find a tick and it's not attached, remove it with a pair of tweezers. If it's attached, use a pair of fine-tipped tweezers or a special tick-removal tool, which helps you remove the tick without squeezing the body. This is important, because you don't want to crush the tick and force disease-carrying saliva or fluids into your puppy's bloodstream. You also don't want to use your fingers, because if you crush the tick while you're touching it, it can also infect you with disease. Don't use petroleum jelly, fingernail polish, or a hot match to try to get the tick to back out. These may cause it to inject more saliva into your puppy's wound, which can transmit more disease.

Grab the tick by the head or mouth parts right where they enter the skin. Do not grab it by its body. You want to be sure to get the entire tick and not leave the mouth attached to your puppy. Pull outward firmly and steadily. Don't twist the tick while you are pulling.

When you've removed the tick, don't flush it down the toilet—this won't kill it. Don't squeeze it, either, because the blood from a

Sarcoptic Mange in Humans

Sarcoptic mange mites will happily chew on you in addition to your puppy. Symptoms for people include an itchy rash, usually along the waistline. If you suspect that you have sarcoptic mange, consult your family physician.

tick can infect you with disease. Instead, drop it in a jar of rubbing alcohol to kill it.

Clean your puppy's bite wound with a disinfectant. You also can apply a little triple antibiotic ointment. Some bite sites may form welts or irritation. This is usually not because you left the tick's head in your puppy but because of the tick's toxic saliva. Talk with your veterinarian if you have any concerns. Jot down the date in case your puppy develops symptoms or illness later.

If you find more than a few ticks on your puppy, it may be more effective to give her an insecticide dip. Consult your veterinarian about which dip is safe for your puppy. Some puppies cannot tolerate very strong insecticides, so always consult your veterinarian before trying one. If you have found ticks and notice that your puppy is shaking her head and pawing at her ear, she also may have a tick latched inside her ear canal. Call your veterinarian for assistance.

Internal Parasites

Internal parasites work from within. Your puppy usually ingests these parasites, which then attack from the inside.

Giardia

Giardia is a protozoan that can be ingested from drinking from contaminated streams, puddles, or other sources. Adult dogs don't always show symptoms, but young puppies are vulnerable. Symptoms include large amounts of watery stools, and weight loss may occur. Treatment includes veterinarian-prescribed medication.

Heartworms

Heartworm is a serious and deadly disease. They are a threat in every state (except Alaska), as well as in other countries. All dogs are susceptible. Thankfully, it's also preventable.

Your puppy can get heartworms after being bitten

Inspect your puppy for fleas and ticks after she's been playing outside.

by a mosquito. The mosquito drinks the blood of an infected animal and ingests the young heartworms, which are called *microfilariae*. In the mosquito, the microfilaria go through three larval stages. The mosquito then transfers the infective third stage larvae to its other victims, such as your puppy. In about one week, the third-stage larvae molt into fourth-stage larvae. As they grow, they move through a dog's body and end up in the heart and blood vessels, where they continue to grow. (Female heartworms can grow up to 14 inches (35.6 cm) long!) After a while, the worms cause damage to the heart and blood vessels, which leads to heart disease, severe lung disease, and damage to other organs. Depending on where the heartworms are, they can cause vessels to clot, liver failure, spontaneous bleeding, and death.

In the early stages of heartworm infestation, your puppy may show no symptoms at all. This is why the vet takes a blood sample from your dog during each annual exam—he wants to try to catch the disease early. As the disease develops, symptoms include coughing, loss of appetite, lethargy, and difficulty breathing. You also may notice your puppy getting tired after just a little bit of exertion. With severe infestations, a dog's ribs will start to show prominently.

The best way to deal with heartworms is to prevent them from infecting your puppy. Talk with your veterinarian about the best treatment, and be sure to administer it faithfully. The most common treatment comes in the form of a pill that you give to your puppy each month. Some liquid treatments also are available, which you apply to your puppy's shoulder blades. Always weigh your growing puppy before giving her the dose. Some puppies may rapidly outgrow the dose that they received the month before, which will still leave them susceptible to heartworms. For example, if your pill is good for dogs up to 30 pounds (13.6 kg) but your puppy now weighs more than this, the pill may not work as effectively.

Treatment for heartworms is serious and

requires veterinary care. Some veterinarians have the skills, training, and equipment to surgically remove adult heartworms, but this usually is reserved for severe infestations. Drugs are a more common choice. The first goal of treatment is to kill the adult worms in your puppy's body and then any microfilariae that may be present. Your dog may have to be hospitalized, because the drugs used to kill heartworms can be very toxic to your puppy. When you bring her home after treatment, ensure that she gets complete rest. This means that you probably will have to crate her for several weeks, only taking her out for potty breaks. Should she be too active, there is a chance that dead heartworms could suddenly dislodge and block vessels in the lungs.

Hookworms

Hookworms are especially prevalent in warm, humid areas of the country. They are small and thin, and measure about ½ inch (1.3 cm) long. They latch onto the mucus lining of a puppy's small intestine and suck blood and tissue, which causes serious blood loss and malnutrition. Hookworms can directly penetrate the skin, usually through the paw pads. Most puppies get these parasites from their mothers.

Symptoms include bloody, dark diarrhea, weight loss, pale mucous membranes from anemia, and weakness. However, adult dogs may not even show symptoms. Very young puppies need immediate veterinary care.

Treatment involves medication from your veterinarian. Because puppies commonly get hookworms from their mothers, they will have several dewormings during their early veterinary examinations. Some heartworm preventive medications also prevent the growth of hookworms.

Roundworms

Roundworms are the most common worm found in dogs. Adult roundworms live in the stomach and intestines and can grow up to 7 inches (17.8 cm) long. Dogs can get roundworms in four ways:

1. Roundworm larvae can pass through the mother's placenta into the unborn puppy. Almost every puppy is infected in this way before birth.
2. Larvae can pass into a puppy through her mother's milk.
3. Puppies and adult dogs can ingest eggs that are in the soil.

Buy Drugs From Your Veterinarian

Some people try to save money by purchasing heartworm preventives, flea preventives, and other drugs on the Internet or at local pet supply stores. Tragically, many of these owners learned the hard way that just because the box looks the same doesn't mean that the drug inside is legitimate.

Don't take a chance with your puppy's health. Always purchase your medications from your veterinarian. You may spend a bit more in prevention, but you'll save a lot of money in veterinary care should your dog become sick from counterfeit medication.

Giardia is a protozoan that can be ingested from drinking from contaminated water sources.

4. Puppies and adult dogs can ingest another carrier of roundworms, such as a rodent.

Roundworms usually don't cause symptoms in adult dogs. In puppies older than 2 months, they may cause vomiting or diarrhea, and you may see the worms in the vomit or feces. They look like white spaghetti strands, and they may move. In very young puppies, roundworms are more serious and can even cause death. Infected puppies may fail to grow well, have a dull coat, suffer from anemia, and often exhibit potbellies.

Treatment involves medication from your veterinarian. Because roundworms are so common that your puppy will have several dewormings during her early veterinary examinations. Some heartworm preventive medication also prevents the growth of roundworms.

People can contract a serious disease called *visceral larva migrans* from ingesting roundworm eggs. This most commonly happens in children under age four who like to eat dirt. If your puppy has been diagnosed with roundworms and you have any concerns about you or your family, please consult your physician.

Tapeworms

Tapeworms can be from about 1 inch (2.5 cm) to several feet (m) long. The head of the worm has hooks and suckers, and it latches onto the wall of the gut. The body is made up of segments. To kill the tapeworm, the head must be killed, or the worm will regenerate itself. Tapeworms lay eggs about ¼ inch (0.6 cm) long that are passed through a dog's feces. You may see them moving around your puppy's anus.

Several different types of tapeworm exist. Your puppy can get one kind by swallowing fleas or lice that have ingested tapeworm eggs. To become infested by other types, your puppy would have to eat an infected rodent, rabbit, sheep, or fish.

Many dogs don't show symptoms of tapeworms. Some may

scratch at their rears or "scoot" on the floor because of the eggs passing through, while some may have abdominal pain.

Treatment involves medication from your veterinarian. You can help to prevent tapeworms by keeping your home free of fleas and lice.

Whipworms

Adult whipworms grow to approximately 1 to 3 inches (2.5 to 7.6 cm) long. They live in the end of a puppy's small intestine and the beginning of the large intestine. The female whipworm doesn't lay as many eggs as other worms, so they can be harder to detect in the stool. Your puppy can get whipworms by ingesting the eggs that another dog has shed.

Symptoms can include severe, chronic diarrhea. Your puppy may strain when she passes her stools, which may contain mucus and blood. With heavy infestations, puppies may develop anemia and lose weight.

Treatment involves medication from your veterinarian. Some heartworm preventive medication also prevents the growth of whipworms.

COMMON DISORDERS AND DISEASES

There is no way to cover all the illnesses that could affect your puppy throughout her life in this book. But some ailments are more common than others. Learn about some of the more common disorders and diseases that your puppy may experience so that you'll be better prepared if she starts showing symptoms.

Allergies

It seems that allergies are becoming more common in puppies. Genetics can play a role; if your puppy's parents had allergies, then she may be likely to have them, too. Certain breeds also seem to be more prone to allergies than others.

An allergy is a reaction caused by exposure to a trigger. The trigger is called an *antigen*. There are three main triggers of dog allergies:

1. Fleas and other biting insects
2. Inhaled antigens, such as dust mites, pollen, grasses, and molds.

If your puppy seems unusually lethargic, take her to the vet.

3. Foods and drugs

How your puppy's body reacts to the antigen is referred to as an *allergic reaction*. For your puppy to have an allergic reaction to something, she must have been exposed to it at least twice. The first time, her body recognizes the item as an intruder and produces antibodies. The second time, her body releases antibodies and histamines to fight the intruder. *Histamines* are what cause the allergic reaction. (That's why *anti*histamines can be effective—they fight histamines.)

Allergies can cause severe reactions in your puppy, enough to make her miserable. And because your puppy is exposed to so many things, it can be hard to figure out what is triggering her allergy. Allergies also can develop years after the first exposure, so something that your puppy has tolerated for a long time can suddenly produce an allergic reaction. If you have a puppy with allergies, you must stock up on patience and work closely with your veterinarian to find out exactly what's causing the problem and how best to treat it.

Dogs usually have skin reactions to allergies. Some are immediate and usually cause hives. The worst kind of immediate reaction, *anaphylactic shock*, is a severe reaction that includes vomiting, diarrhea, difficulty breathing, collapse, and even death. Some reactions are delayed and can cause severe itching.

Flea Allergic Dermatitis

The most common canine allergy, flea allergic dermatitis, occurs when a puppy is allergic to flea saliva.

Symptoms include itching, inflamed skin, and pimple-like welts usually around the rear and base of the tail, under the legs, and in the groin and belly areas. Puppies will chew and scratch themselves. Their fur may fall out, and the skin will become dry and scaly. Sometimes, the skin breaks down and becomes infected and crusty.

Treatment is a multi-step process. Your veterinarian may prescribe antihistamines to help with itching, antibiotics for skin infections, and flea prevention medication. In addition, you must get rid of the fleas on your puppy and in your home and yard, or she will continue to suffer.

Atopic Dermatitis (Canine Atopy)

This is the second most common allergic reaction in dogs. It's a reaction to something that your puppy inhales or absorbs through her skin. It usually develops in puppies and dogs from 1 to 3 years of age. Certain breeds are prone to atopic dermatitis, including Labrador and Golden Retrievers, Poodles, West Highland White Terriers, Boxers, Bulldogs, Lhasa Apsos, Wire Fox Terriers, and English and Irish Setters.

Symptoms first appear with the arrival of weed-pollen season, then can progress to be year-round. In earlier stages, dog may scratch at their ears or under their bellies. They may rub their faces on things, trying to relieve the itch. They also can suffer from watery eyes, sneezing, ear infections, and runny noses. A common symptom is licking of the paws. Some dogs may scratch their skin until it bleeds, experience hair loss, and get crusty skin infections. This is just miserable for a puppy, because she can't get relief from the constant itching.

Treatment involves medication from a veterinarian, who may prescribe antihistamines for itching and antibiotics for skin infections. He also may suggest diet supplements or special shampoos to help bring relief. You may get a referral to a canine

Some puppies are allergic to inhaled antigens, such as grasses.

dermatologist to try and identify which triggers are affecting your puppy.

Food Allergies

The third most common cause of itching and scratching in dogs is food allergy. It can strike dogs of any age. Dogs may be allergic to a variety of foods, including meats, milk, eggs, grains, potatoes, soy, and food additives. These allergies may not cause a reaction for years after a puppy has been eating her food.

Symptoms include severe itching, raised patches of skin, and pimple-like welts, usually on the ears, paws, belly, and backs of the legs. Food allergy is sometimes difficult to diagnose because the symptoms look like those from other allergic reactions.

Treatment involves feeding a hypoallergenic diet and watching for signs of relief. Your veterinarian will recommend a specific brand of food for your puppy. It should be something she hasn't had before, should contain few ingredients, and should be free of preservatives or additives. Switching your puppy from one brand of food to another will probably not work, because many different brands of dog food have common ingredients. It can take several weeks to several months to see a difference in your puppy's symptoms.

Dental Issues

Puppies are born without teeth. Their baby teeth start poking through the gums between two and three weeks of age. At about three months, your puppy will start losing her baby teeth while her adult teeth come in. You may find your puppy's baby teeth in her toys or on the carpet. She may even eat them, but this is normal and shouldn't cause a problem. Adult teeth continue to come in, in stages, until your puppy is about eight months old, at which time the last molars appear. Most adult dogs have 42 teeth.

Retained Baby Teeth

Sometimes baby teeth don't fall out when the adult teeth start coming in. If you see a double row of teeth in your puppy's mouth, this means that she has retained some of her baby teeth. (This is a condition seen more commonly in toy breeds.) It causes the adult teeth to push out of place, which can lead to a bad bite and injuries to the gums. Treatment usually involves removal of the baby teeth by a veterinarian. A convenient time to remove retained baby teeth is when you have your puppy neutered, because she already will be under anesthesia.

One of the most common types of allergy is food allergy.

Periodontal (Gum) Disease

Periodontal disease is one of the most common problems seen in veterinary practices. It's rare for puppies to have it, but starting prevention now is the key to helping your dog avoid it as she grows older. There are two forms of periodontal disease: gingivitis and periodontitis.

In *gingivitis*, tartar builds up around the gum line, causing small pockets that trap food and bacteria. Smaller breeds, and certain breeds such as the Poodle, are very prone to tartar buildup.

Symptoms include bad breath. The gums may be swollen, red, and bleed easily when

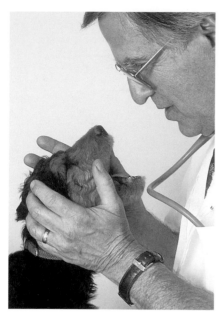

The vet will check your puppy's mouth for retained baby teeth and for signs of dental disease.

touched. You may even see pus if you press along the gum line.

If left untreated, gingivitis turns into *periodontitis*, at which time the gum infection attacks the membrane that holds the teeth in the bone. Teeth become loose and eventually fall out. Root abscesses also may occur, which are very painful. Symptoms include drooling and a reluctance to eat. Treatment involves professional teeth cleaning by your veterinarian. Your dog will be sedated, and the veterinarian will scale and clean her teeth and remove any damaged ones. Some dogs have the disease so badly that they lose most of their teeth. You can help to prevent periodontal disease—and save yourself a good bit of money in dentistry costs—by beginning a good dental care program now. (Refer to Chapter 4 for tips on brushing your dog's teeth.)

In addition to regular brushing, providing your dog with dental chews may help keep his teeth in good condition. Nylabone has a line of chews made specifically for teething puppies.

Ear Infections

Dogs can get a variety of ear infections, caused by either bacteria or yeast. Here are some common causes of ear infections:

- A lot of ear hair, which blocks air circulation.
- Allergies.
- Drop ears. Drop ears don't allow as much air circulation into the ear canal, so they can remain moist or wet, which is a good breeding ground for bacterial or yeast infections.
- Grooming by plucking hair from the ear canals, which can cause sebum to ooze from the hair pores and encourage bacterial growth.
- Narrow ear canals.
- Using a cotton-tipped swab to clean the ears, which can force liquids or bacteria down into the ear canal.
- Water getting into the ears while swimming or bathing.

Symptoms of an ear infection include unusual odor, head shaking, scratching, and rubbing at the ear. The ear will be painful. Your puppy may tilt her head and cry and whine if you touch her ear. The ear will be red and usually have a discharge.

It's important to take your puppy to the veterinarian if you suspect an ear problem. You don't want it to get worse and affect her hearing. The type of ear infection will determine what treatment your veterinarian prescribes. If it progresses too much, the vet may have to sedate her to clean her ears, or he may even have to perform surgery. For a more minor infection, the veterinarian may prescribe medication to put in your puppy's ears. Be sure to follow all directions carefully, and don't touch the tip of the applicator to the ear, or you could contaminate the applicator.

Eye Infections

One of the most common eye problems in dogs is *conjunctivitis*, sometimes called "red eye." Conjunctivitis is an inflammation of the conjunctival membrane that covers the back of the eyelids and the surface of the eyeball, up to the cornea. Symptoms include a red eye with a discharge. Treatment includes an antibiotic ointment.

Conjunctivitis is not painful, so if your puppy is acting as if her eye hurts, she may have another serious problem with her eye. Any time that you suspect an eye problem, it's a good idea to take your puppy to the veterinarian for an examination.

EMERGENCIES

Hopefully, your puppy will sail through life and not experience any emergency health scares. Be prepared for them, however, and you could save her life.

Be very careful when approaching and treating an injured puppy. Even the sweetest dog may bite if she is in pain. If she growls or snaps or if her hackles (the fur on her shoulder blades) are raised, she's trying to tell you that she wants you to leave her alone. Of course, leaving her alone is the last thing you want to do. But she won't understand, because she's hurt and afraid.

In cases like this, it may be necessary to muzzle your puppy. Keep a cloth, soft, or open/basket muzzle on hand in case you need it. You also can get muzzles from your veterinarian or a pet supply store.

If you don't have a muzzle handy, you can get by with a piece of cloth or leash. Tie the cloth around the puppy's muzzle, and then bring the two ends under her ears and tie the ends behind her head.

There are times when you should never muzzle a puppy. These include if she is having difficulty breathing or if she is vomiting, choking, or aggressively resisting the muzzle. Never muzzle an unconscious puppy.

Bites and Stings

A variety of insects, snakes, and other critters can injure your dog. Puppies love to explore, and they don't understand that some things are dangerous. They can easily poke their noses in a fire-ant hill or nudge a sleeping snake. It's important for you to be aware of some common bites and stings and how to treat them.

Insect Stings

Ant, bee, wasp, and yellow jacket stings can cause swelling and redness. The swelling may include the face and neck. If your puppy is stung many times, she could go into shock.

Black widow and brown recluse spider bites are toxic. Symptoms include pain at the site of the bite, excitability, fever, weakness, and muscle and joint pain.

Centipede and scorpion stings cause local reactions and sometimes severe illness.

Here is how to treat a sting:

1. Try to identify the insect. Treatment may depend on what stung your puppy.
2. If you see a bee stinger in your puppy, remove it by scraping it out with a credit card or your fingernail. Don't use tweezers or squeeze it, or you could inject more venom into her.
3. Make a paste of baking soda and a little water, and apply it to the sting site.
4. If practical, apply an ice pack to help reduce swelling.
5. If your puppy becomes agitated, starts scratching at the sting site, begins drooling, has diarrhea or vomiting, or any difficulty breathing, take her to a veterinarian. She could be experiencing deadly anaphylactic shock.

Snake Bites

Both poisonous and nonpoisonous snakes are found in the United States. Most snake bites on dogs occur on the head and legs.

To treat a snake bite, first try to identify the snake. If you are certain that the snake is *not* poisonous, then clean and dress your puppy's wound and consult your veterinarian if you have any concerns. If you know that the snake *is* poisonous, then take the following steps. (Or if you're not sure, it's best to treat your puppy as if the snake was poisonous.)

1. Keep your puppy quiet and as still as possible. Venom will

spread more rapidly if she moves, so if you can, carry your puppy to limit her movement.

2. Do not wash the wound, because this could make the venom enter your puppy's body more.

3. Do not apply ice.

4. Do not make cuts over the wound and try and suck out the venom, like you've seen in the movies. It won't work, and you could ingest the venom, too.

5. Take your puppy to the nearest veterinarian or veterinary emergency clinic for treatment. Do this even if she is not showing any immediate signs; symptoms may be delayed.

If the snake is dead, take it with you for identification. Be very careful! Snakes' fangs can stay venomous for hours after they die, so use caution if you secure the snake to take it for identification.

Bleeding

Seeing blood pour out of your puppy can cause the strongest person to panic, but try to remain calm. She needs your quick action!

The safest way to control bleeding is to apply pressure directly on the wound. Take several sterile gauze squares and put them on the wound. If you don't have sterile gauze, use the cleanest cloths you can find and fold them over thickly. Apply direct pressure for up to ten minutes. Leave the gauze there, and bandage the wound snugly. If you don't have anything to bandage the wound with, keep applying pressure until you can reach a veterinarian. If you see swelling below the bandage, your puppy's circulation is impaired, and you'll need to remove or loosen the bandage.

If your puppy has bright red blood spurting out, then she has arterial bleeding. If you can't control this with direct pressure, use a tourniquet. Use this method only if you can't control the bleeding using direct pressure. You can use tourniquets on your puppy's legs and tail. Always put the tourniquet above the wound, between the wound and the heart. To make a tourniquet,

If an emergency befalls your puppy, put her in the crate and get her to the vet.

Don't allow your puppy to play outside for prolonged periods in cold weather, or she could develop frostbite.

employ the following steps:

1. Use a belt, a piece of cloth, or gauze.
2. Loop the material twice around the area.
3. Twist it with your hands or insert a stick beneath the loop to help you tighten it. Twist until the bleeding stops.
4. Loosen the tourniquet every ten minutes to prevent tissue damage and to check for persistent bleeding.
5. If the bleeding has stopped, apply a direct pressure bandage. If the wound is still bleeding, let it flow for a few seconds and then retwist the tourniquet.

If a wound has stopped bleeding, don't wipe it or pour hydrogen peroxide on it, or you could dislodge the clot.

Your veterinarian can determine if your puppy needs stitches or more intensive care, especially to prevent infection of the wound.

Frostbite

Frostbite occurs when part of the body freezes. Your puppy's ear tips, footpads, and tail are most vulnerable to this emergency condition. Frostbitten skin is pale blue or white at first. As circulation returns, it turns red and swollen and may peel. Eventually, it turns black as the skin dies.

Don't use snow or ice on frostbite, or you could cause more tissue damage. Instead, soak the frostbitten skin in warm—not hot—water for about 20 minutes or until the skin looks flushed.

Do not rub or massage the frostbitten skin. Take your puppy to the veterinarian for further treatment.

As your puppy's skin warms, it could become quite painful for her. She may react out of pain, so restrain her if necessary. Don't let her bite or scratch at the frostbitten spot, or she could cause more damage.

Gastrointestinal Blockages

Puppies lead the pack in swallowing foreign objects. They've been known to ingest golf balls, toys, peach pits, rocks, batteries, jewelry, string, loose change, and more. If you're lucky, your puppy will pass a foreign object, and you'll just find a surprise in her stool. But sometimes the object gets stuck. This is an emergency situation.

Symptoms of a blockage include vomiting, lack of interest in food, lethargy, and pain. The vomit may be projectile or smell like feces. If there is a complete blockage, your puppy will not be able to pass a stool. If you see these signs, take your puppy to a veterinarian right away. She may require surgery to remove the object.

Flat-nosed puppies are more prone to heatstroke than are other breeds.

Heatstroke

Dogs do not sweat; they have to pant to cool themselves. This isn't always very efficient, though, especially in hot weather. A puppy can suffer from heatstroke due to many reasons, including the following:

- She was left in a car in warm weather.
- She exercised in hot, humid weather.
- She was confined in a hot outdoor place without shade.
- She has a flat nose. (Flat-nosed dogs have restricted airways; oxygen doesn't move as well through those narrow nasal passages. It's harder for flat-nosed dogs to breathe in general, so adding a hot environment is even more dangerous.)

• She has a medical condition, such as heart or lung problems.

Symptoms of heatstroke include heavy panting and difficulty breathing. Your puppy's tongue will appear bright red. She may have thick drool and vomit. If it is a severe case, she can go into shock, collapse, and die.

It's very important to treat your puppy quickly. Move her out of the heat and into air conditioning if possible. Take her temperature. If it's above 104°F (40°C) degrees, put her in a bathtub filled with cool water (support her head if she is too weak) or spray her with a garden hose for two minutes. Keep checking her temperature. If it gets to 103°F (39.4°C), stop the cooling techniques. Take her to your veterinarian as soon as possible, even if you get her temperature down. After experiencing heatstroke, dogs can have serious complications, including seizures, heart issues, and kidney failure.

Poisoning

Puppies get into everything. They'll chew on plants that could be poisonous. They don't realize that certain chemicals may be dangerous, especially if they're sweet, like certain medicines. Antifreeze, especially, has a very sweet taste that is appealing to animals, but it's deadly.

If your puppy has swallowed something poisonous, try to identify exactly what she swallowed. Treatment will depend on what she's ingested. Contact a veterinarian right away. (Be sure to have the package with information about the product available.) If your veterinarian is not available, contact your local emergency animal clinic. Or call the National Animal Poison Control Center toll-free at 1-888-426-4435. This service, offered by the American Society for the Prevention of Cruelty to Animals (ASPCA), is available 24 hours a day, 365 days a year. There may be a charge, but it is well worth the price if it saves your puppy's life. The manufacturer also may have a contact phone number or web address on the package, along with toxicity information.

When and How to Induce Vomiting

Your first instinct should your puppy ingest something poisonous may be to get her to throw it up. Wait! Some poisons could actually make your puppy's condition *worse* if you induce vomiting.

Never induce vomiting if:

Too Hot to Handle

On an 85°F (29.4°C) day, it takes just ten minutes for the inside of your car to reach 102°F (38.9°C) — even with the windows cracked. Please, never leave your puppy inside a parked car, not even while you run inside "for just a minute." You could come back a minute too late!

- She's swallowed a sharp object. If she throws it up, it could perforate her stomach or esophagus, or it could become lodged in her airway and choke her.
- She has already vomited.
- She is unconscious, having difficulty breathing, or having seizures.
- She's swallowed an acid, cleaning solution, household chemical, or petroleum product.
- The label on the product says "Do not induce vomiting."

If your veterinarian recommends inducing vomiting, give her 1 teaspoon (4.9 ml) of hydrogen peroxide per 10 pounds (4.5 kg) of her body weight. (Yes, the same hydrogen peroxide that you buy at the drugstore or grocery store.) Repeat about every 15 minutes for up to three doses until she vomits.

HOW TO GIVE MEDICATION

There may be times when you have to give your puppy medication. If you practice these procedures ahead of time and make them pleasant, your puppy is less likely to be afraid or balk at medication later. For practice, you don't actually have to apply any medicine—just go through the motions. Use treats throughout, and praise your puppy for calm behavior.

If you are unsure of how to give your puppy medication, ask your vet to show you.

Ears

Clean and dry your puppy's ears so that the medicine can reach where it needs to go. Gently pull her earflap up and over her head. Insert the end of the medicine dropper or nozzle in the ear but only as far as you can see. Squeeze in the prescribed amount of drops or ointment. Fold her ear flap back over and gently massage the base of her ear to distribute the medicine. You'll probably hear a squishy sound, and that's okay.

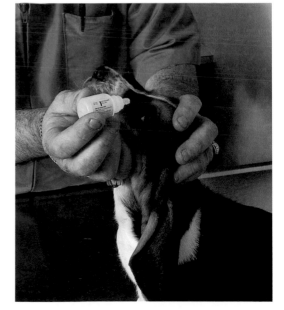

Eyes

To apply eye drops, steady your hand holding the medicine against your puppy's head. Otherwise, drops could splatter everywhere. Use your other hand to gently

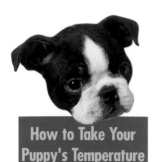

hold your puppy's head still. Tilt her muzzle up, then squeeze the prescribed amount of drops in her eye.

To apply ointment, gently hold your puppy's head still with one hand, using your thumb to draw down her lower eyelid. This will create a little pouch where you want to squeeze the ointment. Steady your hand holding the medicine against her forehead, and be careful if she jerks her head. You don't want to poke her in the eye!

Pills

To give a puppy a pill, the traditional method is to open her jaws, put the pill in the back of her throat, close her mouth, and rub under her neck to make her swallow. In some cases, this can cause puppies to become afraid of your hands. You should teach your puppy to accept your hands in her mouth if you ever have to fish something out of there, but there are also more pleasant ways to administer pills.

Get several marshmallows. For toy or small dogs, you can use miniature marshmallows. Slice one of the marshmallows and put the pill inside, closing the halves together over the pill. Give your puppy a plain marshmallow. Next, give her the one with the pill in it, quickly followed by another plain marshmallow. (Of course, make sure that it's okay to give the specific medication with food before you use this method.)

ALTERNATIVE MEDICINE

Just as people are exploring other forms of health care for themselves, they're also finding success with these methods for their pets. Some people may just be learning about alternative medicine, but most of these treatments have been around for quite some time.

Acupuncture

Acupuncture is a traditional Chinese medicine that has been around for centuries. It involves the use of fine needles inserted into specific parts of the body to stimulate good health. Acupuncture is based on the theory that the life energy that flows from the body's organs can be disturbed by injury or disease. The needles redirect the flow of energy back to more healthful paths.

Acupuncture is used to treat skeletal and muscle problems,

How to Take Your Puppy's Temperature

To take your puppy's temperature, use a rectal thermometer. A digital thermometer is ideal because it's faster, but if you use a bulb thermometer, simply shake it down until it registers 96°F (35.6°C). Lubricate the bulb with petroleum jelly or personal lubricant. Raise your puppy's tail and hold it firmly so she doesn't sit. If possible, have someone occupy your puppy's attention at her head, pet her, and talk to her. Don't reassure her too much, or she'll think that something's wrong. Just praise her for holding still.

Gently insert the bulb into her rectum at least 1 inch (2.5 cm), with a slight twisting motion. Hold the thermometer in place for three minutes. Remove it, wipe it clean, and read the temperature at the highest point of the silver mercury column. Clean it with alcohol after each use. A normal temperature is between 100° and 102°F (37.8° and 38.9°C).

neurological diseases, skin conditions, arthritis, chronic pain, and more. Owners who have canine athletes also use it to help improve competitive performance.

Chiropractic

Chiropractic is a health care profession that focuses on disorders of the muscle, skeletal, and nervous systems. The theory behind chiropractic care is that when these systems are out of alignment, they can affect body function. Chiropractic is used to treat back, muscle, and joint pain. It's a holistic treatment, which also emphasizes the importance of overall health and wellness.

Flower Essences

Dr. Edward Bach, an English physician, developed flower essences to correct emotional imbalances. Flower essences can be used in combination with other therapies, including homeopathy, herbs, and medications. A combination of five of the essences, Rescue Remedy, has been used to relieve extreme stress and fear in animals.

How to Take a Urine Sample

There may be times when your veterinarian needs a urine sample from your puppy. However, your puppy may not be comfortable peeing at the clinic, so learning how to get a sample at home can be convenient.

To prepare, get a clean, plastic container with a snap-on lid that won't leak. You may want to pick up a box of inexpensive, disposable medical gloves from your local drugstore or discount department store. They come in handy for dealing with this and other puppy messes.

Put on your gloves and take your puppy out on leash to pee. You want to be attached to your puppy, because if she's off leash you could end up chasing her all over the yard. Give your puppy the cue to potty.

If you have a male puppy and he lifts his leg to pee, just hold the container in the urine stream. Collecting urine mid-stream is ideal, but don't worry about it if you don't manage to do that. If you have a female puppy or a male who doesn't lift his leg to pee, use the lid of a long, flat plastic container. Make sure that the lid has a lip to it that lets it snap onto the bottom part. When she starts to squat, quickly and quietly slide the lid of the container underneath her. She may startle and stop, but keep trying. The urine will collect in the groove of the lid, and you can then carefully transfer it to the container.

You don't need to get all the urine, and you don't need to fill the container completely. Snap on the lid, and clean the outside of the container. You can keep a urine sample for up to 30 minutes at room temperature before it needs to be tested. If you can't work within that timeframe, refrigerate the sample.

Herbal

Herbal treatments are used to treat a variety of problems, from carsickness to arthritis pain. Some, such as glucosamine, have scientific studies behind them to prove their effectiveness. Just because they are natural, however, doesn't mean they are nontoxic. If you are considering herbal treatment for your puppy, consult a specialist first. Always let your veterinarian know of any herbal supplements your puppy takes, because some may not combine well with certain medications.

Homeopathy

Homeopathic medicine is medicine that determines the underlying energy pattern of an animal and analyzes what can be done to bring the energy back into balance. The goal of homeopathy is not just to address the symptoms of a disease but to address all changes in the energy balance of an animal. Homeopathic remedies are extremely diluted solutions of herbs, animal products, and chemicals. If you are considering homeopathic treatment for your puppy, always consult a specialist first. Tell your veterinarian about any treatments that your puppy may be taking, because they may not combine well with other medications.

When Should You Call the Vet?

Puppies have ups and downs when it comes to their health, and this is normal. For example, it's not uncommon for puppies to experience mild diarrhea or vomiting once in a while. How do you know when it's serious enough to call the vet? Look for these signs and symptoms as a clue to get help:

- abnormal discharge from anywhere
- difficulty getting up or down
- difficulty peeing or pooping
- excessive diarrhea or vomiting
- head shaking, excessive scratching, or licking
- limping
- lumps or swelling
- reduced or increased appetite or water consumption
- significant weight loss or gain

Massage

Massage is the practice of applying pressure or vibration to the soft tissues of the body. It encourages healing by promoting blood flow, relieving tension, loosening muscles, and stimulating nerves. It's used to ease pain and help improve muscle tone, and it can be a great way to get your puppy used to handling. Owners who have canine athletes also use it to help ease muscles during training and competition.

A healthy puppy has clear, bright eyes and a glossy coat.

If you'd like to learn how to massage your puppy, find a professional to teach you. Massage should feel good to your puppy. Stop if she becomes agitated or doesn't enjoy the massage.

You and your puppy are just starting your lives together. You have many adventures ahead!

Adolescence can be a difficult time. When your puppy enters the equivalent of her teen years, you may find it a bit trying. You may see some behavioral issues pop up, and your puppy may forget some of her training. But stick with it. If you work on building a solid foundation now, all your work will pay off in a lasting relationship.

Take lots of pictures now. She'll only be a puppy once! You'll treasure them as you look back on this time. Best wishes with your new family companion.

Chocolate Isn't so Sweet

Chocolate is poisonous to dogs. The darker the chocolate, the higher the amount of chemicals that can hurt your puppy. Baking chocolate is the most dangerous. So stick to dog treats for your puppy, and keep the chocolate for yourself!

CHOOSING THE PERFECT PUPPY FOR YOU

Everybody loves puppies, and nothing can be more cuddly and charming. They are so adorable that it's easy to forget all your careful plans and bring home the first little fluffball who greets you with sweet eyes and a wagging tail. Resist the temptation!

Take your time and figure out exactly what you want and need in a puppy. Then, purchase or adopt your puppy from a reliable, quality source. Your goal is to find a healthy, happy, friendly puppy—not one with serious health or dangerous behavioral issues. Do your homework ahead of time, and you'll help save yourself from big veterinary bills and a broken heart.

What's Your Idea of a Perfect Puppy?

Everyone has their own idea of the type of puppy that would best fit into their hearts and homes. Make a list of what you want in a dog, and then research different breeds to see if they match your list. Be realistic. For example, if you know that you couldn't live with a yappy dog, it's best not to choose a breed known for being talkative, such as a Shetland Sheepdog. If your busy schedule will not allow you to adequately exercise an active puppy, you should probably avoid most of the sporting breeds, like Golden or Labrador Retrievers.

To learn more about breeds, read books, talk to veterinarians and professional dog trainers, and consult breed rescue groups. If you're thinking about a mixed-breed puppy, study the combinations of breeds because your puppy will inherit traits from each. Ask about the good points and bad points of each breed you're considering to get a complete picture.

Building Blocks That Make a Great Puppy

With a puppy, you can ensure from the start that she's getting the right training, the right nutrition, and the right health care. But just as you need quality clay to shape beautiful pottery, you need a good puppy to make a great dog. Here are some important building blocks to look for.

Great Parents

Every purebred dog is prone to genetic diseases. For example, Labrador Retrievers are prone to hip dysplasia, Yorkshire Terriers are susceptible to Cushing's disease—and the list goes on and on. Fortunately, dogs can be tested for many of these diseases, and those who have them should not be bred. Once you decide what kind of puppy you want, research the diseases that she could possibly inherit and make sure that her breeder has tested against them. It's not a guarantee that your puppy won't get a genetic disease, but it betters her chances if her line is free of them.

Your puppy's parents also greatly influence your puppy's temperament. A shy, fearful mother is likely to have shy, fearful puppies. An aggressive dad is likely to father aggressive puppies. As a result, some puppies can be genetically prone to shyness, fearfulness, or aggression. No amount of love or training can undo DNA. You can try to reshape behavior, but it will be a challenging project.

It's important to meet at least one of your puppy's parents so that you can get a good picture of her future temperament. Don't accept excuses, such as "Oh she's growling because she had a bad day. She's normally a pussycat!" If a mother or father dog is aggressive or shy, look elsewhere for your puppy.

If you are adopting your puppy from a rescue organization, you may not get a chance to meet a parent. Ask if anything is known about the parents to help you get a better idea of your puppy's health and temperament heritage.

Great Socialization

To get a good start in life, a puppy needs a lot of positive socialization experiences. The critical period for puppies to be influenced by their environments is up to 16 weeks of age. A good breeder or rescue organization will make sure that a young puppy meets a wide variety of people, gets exposed to different surfaces and textures, is handled all over her body, and enjoys all her experiences. This will help to build a confident, outgoing puppy.

THE SOURCE
Breeders

If you have decided that a purebred dog is right for you, first find a reputable breeder. Each breed has a parent breed club, which can provide you with a list of their breeders. It is very important that the puppy be purchased from a breeder who has earned a reputation for consistently producing dogs who are physically healthy and mentally sound. Breeders earn that reputation by breeding their dogs selectively.

Questions to Ask Before Purchasing a Puppy From a Breeder

1. **What are your breeding priorities?** The breeder should aim for excellent health, friendly temperament, and a sound structure.

2. **Are you a member of any breed club?**
   The breeder should be actively involved in his particular breed's club.

3. **What health tests have you done on the parents of the litter and/or the puppies? Can I see documentation of those tests?** The breeder should have had both parents checked for a variety of health issues, such as hip dysplasia, elbow dysplasia, eye disease, and heart defects. Always ask to see the test results—you can even verify some on the Internet. Don't take a breeder's word only. A quality breeder will gladly back up her health statements with documentation.

4. **What veterinary care has the puppy received so far?** Puppies should have had at least one and preferably two sets of complete vaccinations and a worming by eight weeks. (This also can depend on the breed.) The breeder should have complete documentation of these and any other veterinary care the puppies have received.

5. **How soon can I take home a puppy?** You should not be able to take a puppy home before she is eight weeks of age. With some toy breeds, it's not uncommon to wait until 12 weeks. A breeder who wants to give you a puppy earlier may not understand the importance of litter socialization and early puppy learning, which is not a good indication.

6. **What kind of guarantees do you offer? Do I have to sign a contract?** The breeder should offer a contract that protects both him and you. The contract should require that you have the puppy examined by a vet within 48 hours. It may also state that you will not receive registration papers on the puppy until you show proof of neutering, which is a very common practice for nonshow puppies. This indicates that the breeder is careful about his breeding program, which is a positive sign.

7. **Is the puppy registered?** It's a common misconception that a pedigree (a written record of a dog's lineage) from an official registry is a sign of quality or a stamp of approval. It's not. A pedigree is just supposed to be an indication that both parents are purebred and of the same breed. It doesn't mean that the parents are healthy or have stable temperaments.

   That said, it's still a good idea to find a breeder who registers her dogs. Dogs who are registered with the American Kennel Club (AKC), Canadian Kennel Club (CKC), or Kennel Club may be more likely to come from breeders who are following certain standards, but it's not a guarantee. Avoid registries with no standards that will register any dog without proof of a pedigree.

8. **Can you provide references?** The breeder should provide a list of references, including one from his veterinarian.

Rescue Organizations and Shelters

Some rescue groups and shelters are responsible and some are not, just as with every other source for finding a puppy.

When interviewing organizations, ask for references from their veterinarians and others who have adopted from them. Just as with breeders, they should not be willing to give up a puppy until she is at least eight weeks old. They also should use formal contracts.. Nearly all rescue groups will include a clause that if the puppy doesn't work out for you, you must return her to the rescue organization. You cannot simply resell her or give her away. Most rescue organizations also require a home visit before they will allow you to adopt one of their puppies. The puppies they deal with have already had a rough start in life. Rescue groups want to make sure that your home will be the puppy's forever home.

Just as you would probably have to wait for a puppy from a breeder, you may have to wait for a rescue also. This will depend on the availability of the puppy, your willingness to travel, and your specific needs. Some people manage to get their rescue puppy in just a couple of weeks. Others have waited years. She'll be worth the wait!

Questions to Ask the Rescue Organization or Shelter

1. **How did this puppy end up in shelter/rescue?** Many puppies end up in shelters and rescue organizations through no fault of their own. Their owners may have moved and couldn't take their pets. Perhaps the mother dog got pregnant and the owner didn't want to deal with puppies. Often, people make the wrong choice in the type of puppy they bring home and simply change their minds. On the other hand, some puppies may have been given up because of problem behaviors.

2. **How old is the puppy? How is her health? Can you tell me anything about her parents? What is her temperament like?** Ideally, you will adopt a healthy puppy who is at least eight weeks old, with a friendly, outgoing temperament. If the parent or parents are also at the rescue organization, be sure to meet them, too.

3. **Will you take the puppy back if she isn't a good fit in my home?** A quality rescue organization or shelter will readily take the puppy back.

Other Sources

If you are tempted to get a puppy from another source, such as a pet store or flea market, ask them all the questions that you would of a breeder or rescue organization. If they can't give you good answers, don't have written contracts, or do not have health documentation, look elsewhere for your puppy. It may take you a bit longer, but you'll be happy that you waited for the right puppy to come along.

The Puppy

Once you've decided on a quality source for your puppy, picking her out is the fun part. Take your time and resist the urge to smuggle them all home. You want to make the right choice for you.

Parents

Start with the parents, if possible. If there are any temperament problems or if you just don't like them, don't even bother looking at the puppies, because it'll be that much harder to go home without one. Remember, parents are a great predictor of how your puppy will grow up.

Appearance

The eyes and ears of the puppy should be clear and free of discharge, and the coat and skin should have a clean, healthy appearance. The gums should be a healthy pink color, not pale or red. There should not be any external parasites, such as fleas or ticks. Although young puppies do not have much coordination, they should still be able to move well. If you see a puppy limping, favoring a leg, or having trouble moving while the others are moving quite well, there may be a health issue or injury.

Temperament

The puppy who is the first to charge up to you, knocking her brothers and sisters over to get there, is likely a very assertive puppy. This is not the best choice for the typical family. (If you're looking for a competitive athlete, however, she could be a good candidate.) The puppy who runs away at the sight of you or who hides from you is likely a very shy puppy. You may be tempted to "save" her, but this is also not a good typical choice. Shy puppies can develop aggression issues because they are frightened of their environments. You want a puppy who is friendly and outgoing, without being aggressive.

See how the puppies play together. Do they get along? Is one a bully? Avoid that one! Take a toy and interact with the group of puppies. Do they want to play with you? Examine a puppy by herself, preferably in a separate room. Squat or sit down and call her to you. She should come happily and not be afraid of you. Pick her up gently and rub her ears and paws. It's okay if she's a bit squirmy, but she should appear to enjoy your touch. If she gets overly agitated or starts to cry out, she may not have had much handling.

Happily Ever After

Does all this seem overwhelming? Don't hesitate to ask for help. Contact a professional dog trainer to examine the puppies with you. She can point out concerns and help you learn how to better read puppy behavior to help you make your choice. Choosing a puppy is a big decision—one you'll live with for a puppy's lifetime. Just think of the satisfaction and joy you'll have when you finally bring that one, special puppy home.

ASSOCIATIONS AND ORGANIZATIONS

REGISTRIES

American Kennel Club (AKC)
5580 Centerview Drive
Raleigh, NC 27606
Telephone: (919) 233-9767
Fax: (919) 233-3627
E-mail: info@akc.org
www.akc.org

Canadian Kennel Club (CKC)
89 Skyway Avenue, Suite 100
Etobicoke, Ontario M9W 6R4
Telephone: (416) 675-5511
Fax: (416) 675-6506
E-mail: information@ckc.ca
www.ckc.ca

The Kennel Club
1 Clarges Street
London
W1J 8AB
Telephone: 0870 606 6750
Fax: 0207 518 1058
www.the-kennel-club.org.uk

United Kennel Club (UKC)
100 E. Kilgore Road
Kalamazoo, MI 49002-5584
Telephone: (269) 343-9020
Fax: (269) 343-7037
E-mail: pbickell@ukcdogs.com
www.ukcdogs.com

RESCUE ORGANIZATIONS AND ANIMAL WELFARE GROUPS

American Humane Association (AHA)
63 Inverness Drive East
Englewood, CO 80112
Telephone: (303) 792-9900
Fax: 792-5333
www.americanhumane.org

American Society for the Prevention of Cruelty to Animals (ASPCA)
424 E. 92nd Street
New York, NY 10128-6804
Telephone: (212) 876-7700
www.aspca.org

Royal Society for the Prevention of Cruelty to Animals (RSPCA)
Telephone: 0870 3335 999
Fax: 0870 7530 284
www.rspca.org.uk

The Humane Society of the United States (HSUS)
2100 L Street, NW
Washington DC 20037
Telephone: (202) 452-1100
www.hsus.org

SPORTS

American Kennel Club
Agility: www.akc.org/events/agility/index.cfm
Conformation: www.akc.org/events/conformation/index.cfm
Obedience: www.akc.org/events/obedience/index.cfm
AKC Rally®: www.akc.org/events/rally/index.cfm

Association of Pet Dog Trainers (APDT) Rally
E-mail: rallyo@apdt.com
www.apdt.com/po/rally/default.aspx

International Agility Link (IAL)
E-mail: yunde@powerup.au
www.agilityclick.com/~ial

North American Flyball Association (NAFA)
E-mail: flyball@flyball.org
www.flyball.org

VETERINARY RESOURCES

Academy of Veterinary Homeopathy (AVH)
P.O. Box 9280
Wilmington, DE 19809
Telephone: (866) 652-1590
Fax: (866) 652-1590
E-mail: office@TheAVH.org
www.theavh.org

American Animal Hospital Association (AAHA)
P.O. Box 150899
Denver, CO 80215-0899
Telephone: (303) 986-2800
Fax: (303) 986-1700
E-mail: info@aahanet.org
www.aahanet.org/index.cfm

American Holistic Veterinary Medical Association (AHVMA)
2218 Old Emmorton Road
Bel Air, MD 21015
Telephone: (410) 569-0795
Fax: (410) 569-2346

E-mail: office@ahvma.org
www.ahvma.org

American Veterinary Medical Association (AVMA)
1931 North Meacham Road – Suite 100
Schaumburg, IL 60173
Telephone: (847) 925-8070
Fax: (847) 925-1329
E-mail: avmainfo@avma.org
www.avma.org

British Veterinary Association (BVA)
7 Mansfield Street
London
W1G 9NQ
Telephone: 020 7636 6541
Fax: 020 7436 2970
E-mail: bvahq@bva.co.uk
www.bva.co.uk

TRAINING AND BEHAVIOR RESOURCES

Animal Behavior Society (ABS)
Certified Applied Animal Behaviorist Directory:
www.animalbehavior.org/ABSAppliedBehavior/caab-directory

Association of Pet Dog Trainers (APDT)
150 Executive Center Drive
Box 35
Greenville, SC 29615
Telephone: (800) PET-DOGS
Fax: (864) 331-0767
E-mail: information@apdt.com
www.apdt.com

Certification Council for Professional Dog Trainers (CCPDT)
E-mail: administrator@ccpdt.org
www.ccpdt.org

ANIMAL-ASSISTED ACTIVITIES & THERAPY ORGANIZATIONS

Delta Society
875 124th Ave NE, Suite 101
Bellevue, WA 98005
Telephone: (425) 226-7357
Fax: (425) 235-1076
E mail: info@deltasociety.org
www.deltasociety.org

Therapy Dogs International (TDI)
88 Bartley Road
Flanders, NJ 07836
Telephone: (973) 252-9800
Fax: (973) 252-7171
E-mail: tdi@gti.net
www.tdi-dog.org

PUBLICATIONS

BOOKS

Anderson, Teoti. *The Super Simple Guide to Housetraining.* Neptune City: T.F.H. Publications, Inc., 2004.

———. *Quick & Easy Crate Training.* Neptune City: T.F.H. Publications, Inc., 2005.

———. *Your Outta Control Puppy.* Neptune City: T.F.H. Publications Inc., 2003.

Lane, Dick, and Neil Ewart. *A-Z of Dog Diseases & Health Problems.* New York: Howell Books, 1997.

Rubenstein, Eliza, and Shari Kalina. *The Adoption Option: Choosing and Raising the Shelter Dog for You.* New York: Howell Books, 1996.

MAGAZINES

AKC Family Dog
American Kennel Club
260 Madison Avenue
New York, NY 10016
Telephone: (800) 490-5675
E-mail: familydog@akc.org
www.akc.org/pubs/familydog

AKC Gazette
American Kennel Club
260 Madison Avenue
New York, NY 10016
Telephone: (800) 533-7323
E-mail: gazette@akc.org
www.akc.org/pubs/gazette

Dog & Kennel
Pet Publishing, Inc.
7-L Dundas Circle
Greensboro, NC 27407
Telephone: (336) 292-4272
Fax: (336) 292-4272
E-mail: info@petpublishing.com
www.dogandkennel.com

INDEX

Note: Boldfaced numbers indicate illustrations.

ACKNOWLEDGMENTS

My heartfelt gratitude goes to my family, Mami, Dadi, Marci, Rob, Tata, and Uncle Bob. No matter where this dog-related road has taken me, their love and support has always followed. Special thanks to my wonderful Pawsitive Results Support Team, Phyllis Beasley and Jenny Marbach, for their friendship and dedication to helping dogs and their families. I sincerely appreciate my editor, Stephanie Fornino, and the great folks at T.F.H. Publications, Inc., for their collaborative efforts. To Dr. Ian Dunbar and Dr. Patricia McConnell—thank you for teaching me better ways to communicate with my canine friends. My thanks also to the Association of Pet Dog Trainers for helping train the trainer. And to all the puppies and their families who have come through my classes, there just aren't enough cookies for all you've given me.

ABOUT THE AUTHOR

Teoti Anderson, CPDT, is a Certified Pet Dog Trainer and the owner of Pawsitive Results, L.L.C., in Lexington, South Carolina (www.getpawsitiveresults.com). A professional dog trainer for more than 13 years, she is the author of *Your Outta Control Puppy, The Super Simple Guide to Housetraining,* and the Dog Writers Association of America award-winning *Quick & Easy Crate Training.* Teoti is past president of the Association of Pet Dog Trainers and enjoys visiting local health care facilities with her Labrador Retriever and cat. She serves as a training consultant to rescue organizations and gives canine behavior and instructor presentations at conferences across the country.

PHOTO CREDITS

Photo on page 4 courtesy of Shawn Hine (Shutterstock).

Photo on page 23 courtesy of Stephen Walls (Shutterstock).

Photo on page 30 courtesy of Naomi Hasegawa (Shutterstock).

Photo on page 35 courtesy of Steven Pepple (Shutterstock).

Photo on page 49 courtesy of James Stuart Griffith (Shutterstock).

Photo on page 52 courtesy of Paulette Braun.

Photo on page 62 courtesy of Judy Ben Joud (Shutterstock).

Photos on pages 108 and 110 courtesy of pixshots (Shutterstock).

Photo on page 140 courtesy of George Lee (Shutterstock).

Photo on page 180 courtesy of Tootles (Shutterstock).

Author photo on page 207 courtesy of Kim Truett.

All other photos courtesy of Isabelle Francais and T.F.H. archives.

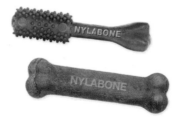
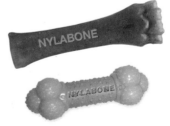